Math Skills Workout

Grade 1

About This Book

Use this super resource—*Math Skills Workout Grade 1*—to help get your youngsters' math skills in tip-top shape! The two-page activities in *Math Skills Workout Grade 1* are designed to reinforce previously introduced math concepts. Each activity has a colorful teacher page and a skill-based reproducible student page.

The teacher page includes the following:
- the purpose of the activity
- a summary of what students will do
- a list of all needed materials, including any provided patterns
- vocabulary to review before the students complete the reproducible
- two fun-filled extension activities

The student page is a skill-based reproducible that supports NCTM standards. Each reproducible has a bonus box designed to provide an extra challenge. Any needed answer keys are found at the end of the book.

Choose from more than 75 two-page activities to meet your students' needs. Then use the accompanying extension ideas to give your youngsters extra skill reinforcement or to informally assess their progress. Tailoring math practice has never been so easy!

www.themailbox.com

TEC837.   The Best of *The Mailbox*® Math • Grades 1–3
TEC881.   The Best of *Teacher's Helper*® Math • Book 1 • Grade 1
TEC3211.   The Best of *Teacher's Helper*® Math • Book 2 • Grade 1

Project Manager: Amy Erickson
Staff Editors: Denine T. Carter, Diane F. McGraw, Deborah G. Swider
Copy Editors: Sylvan Allen, Gina Farago, Karen Brewer Grossman,
  Karen L. Huffman, Amy Kirtley-Hill, Debbie Shoffner
Cover Artist: Clevell Harris
Art Coordinator: Clevell Harris
Artists: Cathy Spangler Bruce, Pam Crane, Theresa Lewis Goode, Nick
  Greenwood, Clevell Harris, Sheila Krill, Mary Lester, Clint Moore,
  Kimberly Richard, Greg D. Rieves, Rebecca Saunders, Barry Slate,
  Donna K. Teal
Typesetters: Lynette Dickerson, Mark Rainey

President, The Mailbox Book Company™: Joseph C. Bucci
Director of Book Planning and Development: Chris Poindexter
Book Development Managers: Stephen Levy, Elizabeth H. Lindsay,
  Thad McLaurin, Susan Walker
Curriculum Director: Karen P. Shelton
Traffic Manager: Lisa K. Pitts
Librarian: Dorothy C. McKinney
Editorial and Freelance Management: Karen A. Brudnak
Editorial Training: Irving P. Crump
Editorial Assistants: Terrie Head, Melissa B. Montanez,
  Hope Rodgers, Jan E. Witcher

©2001 THE EDUCATION CENTER, INC.
All rights reserved.
ISBN #1-56234-468-4

Table of Contents

Number and Operations

Measurement

Geometry

Algebraic Concepts

Probability, Statistics, and Graphing

Problem Solving

Strike Up the Ordinal Number Band!

Count on this "sound-sational" activity to keep youngsters in step with ordinal numbers!

Purpose: To identify ordinal positions through 12th

Students will do the following:

- sequence ordinal numbers through 12th
- identify given ordinal number words

Materials for each student:

- copy of page 6
- pencil
- crayons
- glue
- scissors

Vocabulary to review:

- ordinal number

Extension activities to use after the reproducible:

- Try this small-group game of number-order hide-and-seek! Turn 12 disposable cups upside down and then label the cups with ordinal number words *first* through *twelfth*. Stand the cups in a horizontal line and secretly place an object under a chosen cup. To play one round, a volunteer guesses under which cup the object is hidden by asking a question that includes a position and an ordinal number word, such as "Is the object *before* the *seventh* cup?" After you answer the question, invite other students to make guesses in a similar manner until the object's correct position is identified. The student who identifies it hides the object and answers the questions in the next round.

- Students draw on their ordinal number skills with this picture-perfect activity! On a sheet of story paper, each student illustrates his family members standing in a line. He labels each person with an ordinal number that describes the member's pictured position. Then, below the illustration, the youngster writes a sentence about each family member, being sure to use an ordinal number word. Compile and bind youngsters' completed work in a class album titled "Family Order Fun."

Strike Up the Ordinal Number Band!

Help the animals finish getting ready for the parade!
Color. Cut out the hats.
Glue each hat on the correct animal.

| eleventh 11th | second 2nd | sixth 6th | third 3rd | eighth 8th |
| fifth 5th | tenth 10th | ninth 9th | first 1st | twelfth 12th |

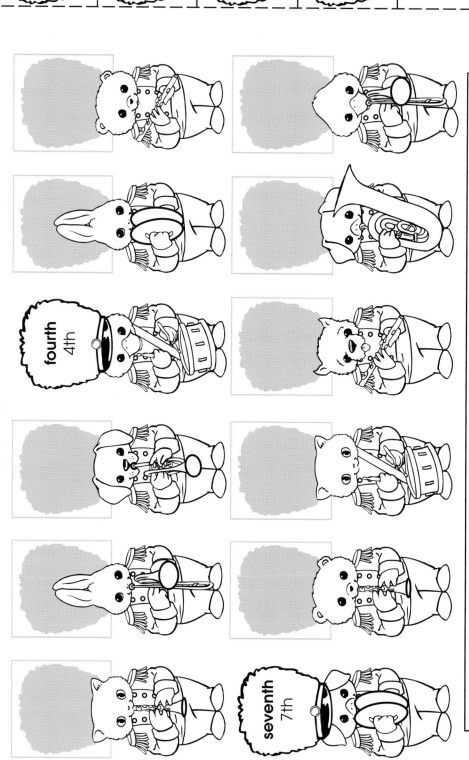

fourth 4th

seventh 7th

Bonus Box: Draw an X above the fourth animal. On the back of this sheet, write a sentence that tells what instrument it is playing.

©2001 The Education Center, Inc. • *Math Skills Workout* • TEC3225 • Key p. 167

"Misssing" Numbers

Take the mystery out of number order with these wriggly critters!

Purpose: To order and compare numbers to 99

Students will do the following:

- write the missing numbers in ascending order
- classify sets of numbers as greater or less than 50

Materials for each student:

- copy of page 8
- pencil
- green crayon
- brown crayon

Vocabulary to review:

- number series
- missing number
- greater than
- less than

Extension activities to use after the reproducible:

- Use this "sssuper" center for number-order practice! Draw a snake shape along the length of a sentence strip. Use a marker to divide the shape into several sections and then program each section with a consecutive numeral from a chosen number series. Cut out the sections. Code the back of each one for self-checking. Store the resulting snake puzzle in a resealable plastic bag in a center. Use a different color of marker to program each additional puzzle that you make. Have a student remove the sections from one bag, assemble the snake by sequencing the numbers, and then flip the sections to check her work.

- Put your young sleuths on the case of the mystery number! Pair students and give each youngster a laminated copy of the hundred chart (page 159), a file folder, and a wipe-off marker. One player in each twosome uses his folder to conceal his chart. Then he marks a chosen number. His partner tries to identify the number by asking yes or no questions such as "Is the number between 10 and 20?" After each response, the partner marks the number(s) on his board that can be eliminated. After he identifies the number, the players erase their charts, trade roles, and play again.

Comparing and ordering numbers 7

"Misssing" Numbers

Write the missing numbers.
Use the color code to outline each snake.

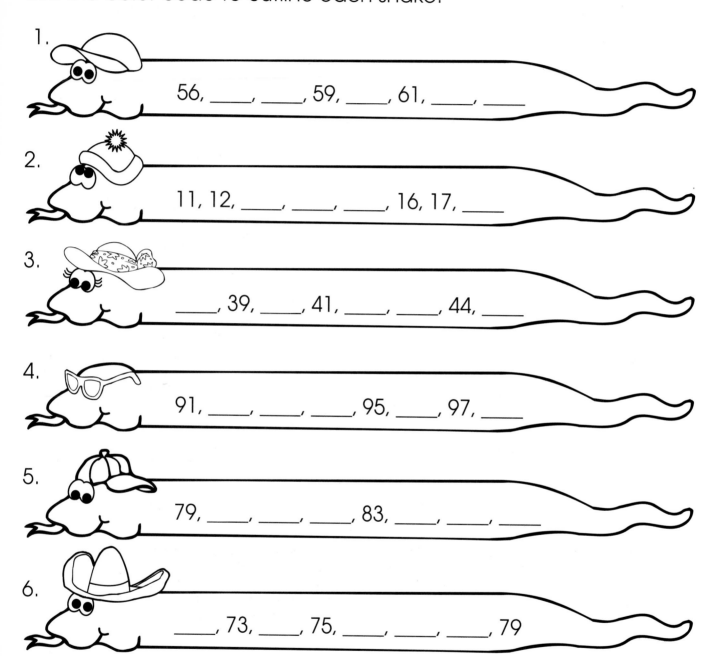

1. 56, ____, ____, 59, ____, 61, ____, ____

2. 11, 12, ____, ____, ____, 16, 17, ____

3. ____, 39, ____, 41, ____, ____, 44, ____

4. 91, ____, ____, ____, 95, ____, 97, ____

5. 79, ____, ____, ____, 83, ____, ____, ____

6. ____, 73, ____, 75, ____, ____, ____, 79

Color Code
Green: numbers <u>greater than</u> 50
Brown: numbers <u>less than</u> 50

Bonus Box: Look at number 2. On the back of this sheet, write the next ten numbers in the series.

Order Up!

Students are sure to work up an appetite for number order
with this tantalizing reproducible!

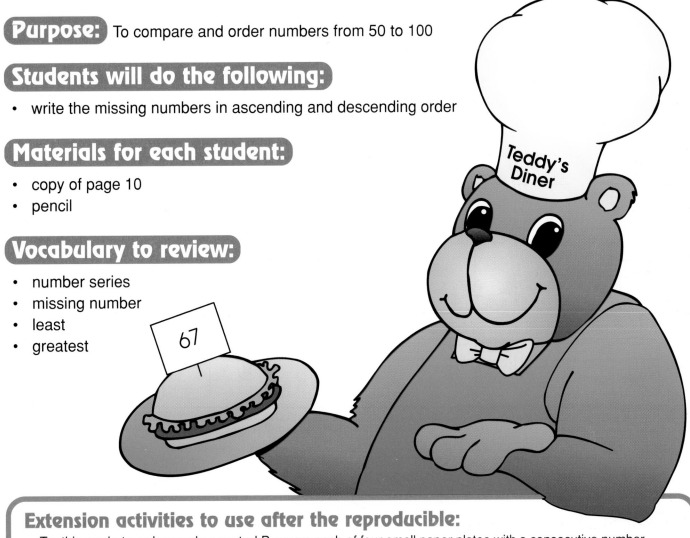

Purpose: To compare and order numbers from 50 to 100

Students will do the following:

- write the missing numbers in ascending and descending order

Materials for each student:

- copy of page 10
- pencil

Vocabulary to review:

- number series
- missing number
- least
- greatest

67

Extension activities to use after the reproducible:

- Try this made-to-order number center! Program each of four small paper plates with a consecutive number from a chosen number series and then code the back of each for self-checking. Prepare a second set of plates with a different number series. Scramble the plates, tuck them inside a resealable plastic bag, and place the bag at a center. A student removes the plates, sorts them by the number series, and then sequences the plates in each series. After she writes each number series on provided paper, she flips the plates over to check her work.

- Brighten up number-order practice! Copy a class set plus one extra of the hundred chart (page 159). Color a multicolored picture or design on one chart. Write on the board the name of one color in the illustration. For each numbered box of that color, write the numbers that come immediately before and after. (For example, for 43 write "42 __ 44.") Give each student one copy of the blank hundred chart. The student determines which numbers are missing from the listed series and colors the corresponding boxes as indicated. Later, repeat the activity for the remaining colors. Then have students compare their completed illustrations with yours.

1	2	3	4	5	6	7	8	9	10
11	12	13	14	15	16	17	18	19	20
21	22	23	24	25	26	27	28	29	30
31	32	33	34	35	36	37	38	39	40
41	42	43	44	45	46	47	48	49	50
51	52	53	54	55	56	57	58	59	60
61	62	63	64	65	66	67	68	69	70
71	72	73	74	75	76	77	78	79	80
81	82	83	84	85	86	87	88	89	90
91	92	93	94	95	96	97	98	99	100

Order Up!

Write the missing numbers. *(Hint: Count down for some sets.)*

1. 86 87 ___ ___ 90 ___ ___ 93 ___

Today's Special

2. ___ 55 ___ ___ 52 ___

3. 74 ___ 76 ___ ___ ___ 80

4. 71 ___ 69 68 ___ ___

Now **follow** the directions below.

For each number series, **circle** the greatest number. **Draw** an X on the smallest number.

Bonus Box: On the back of this sheet, write the following numbers in order from <u>least</u> to <u>greatest</u>: 82, 57, 100, 86, 60, 75, 93.

©2001 The Education Center, Inc. • *Math Skills Workout* • TEC3225 • Key p. 167

Odd and Even Racers

Rev up odd and even number recognition!

Purpose: To identify odd and even numbers

Students will do the following:

- count sets of shapes and write each corresponding number
- determine if numbers are odd or even
- use labels to classify numbers as odd or even

Materials for each student:

- copy of page 12
- pencil
- red crayon
- blue crayon
- scissors
- glue

Vocabulary to review:

- odd
- even

Extension activities to use after the reproducible:

- Pair up manipulatives and math fun with this partner activity! Remind students that an even number has a "buddy" and an odd number does not. Give each pair of students a sheet of paper and 20 counters. One student in each twosome divides the paper into two columns and labels one column "odd" and the other "even." To begin play, one student sets a number of counters in front of his partner. The partner pairs the counters, determines if the amount is odd or even, and then records the number in the appropriate column. The partners switch roles and continue play until each partner has had five turns pairing the counters.

- Head outside for a game of The Odd Man Wins! Choose one student to be It. He stands in a central location, closes his eyes, and says "Go!" At this signal, the remaining students randomly arrange themselves into small groups by linking arms as the student who is It slowly counts to ten. When the student who is It reaches ten, he calls out either "odd" or "even." Each group that has a corresponding quantity of students goes to the side to sit out. The game continues for a desired period of time or until no groups remain.

12

Odd and Even Racers

Count the shapes . **Write** how many.
Color the even cars red. **Color** the odd cars blue.
Cut out each driver.
Glue him onto a matching car.

Bonus Box: Write the numbers 1–10 on the back of this sheet. Use a red crayon to circle each even number. Use a blue crayon to circle each odd number. Look at your work. Write a sentence that tells what you see.

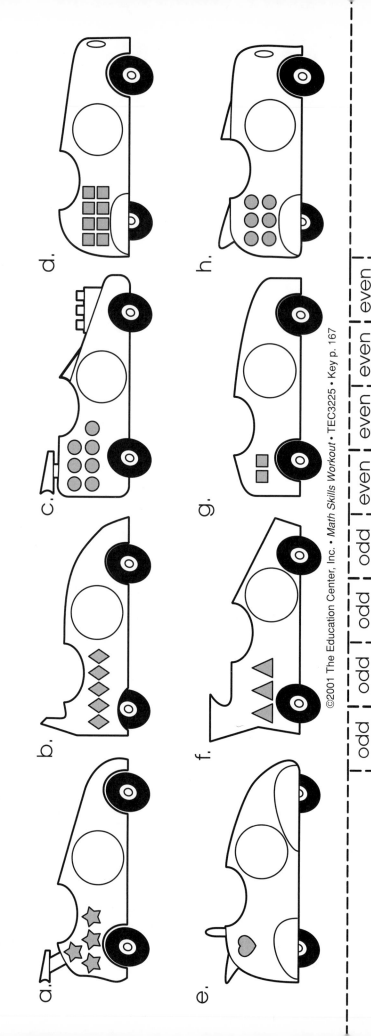

a.

b.

c.

d.

e.

f.

g.

h.

even even even even odd odd odd odd

Popcorn, Anyone?

Serve up this poppin' fresh place-value practice and count on your students to ask for more!

Purpose: To count and rewrite sets of tens and ones

Students will do the following:

- use a pictorial key
- count sets of tens and ones
- rewrite sets of tens and ones

Materials for each student:

- copy of page 14
- pencil

Vocabulary to review:

- key
- tens
- ones
- set

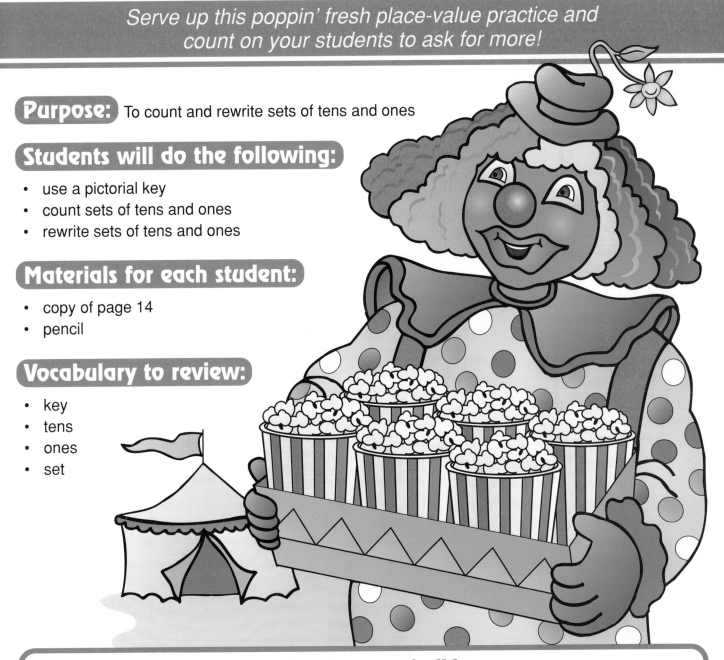

Extension activities to use after the reproducible:

- This tantalizing place-value activity hits the spot! Pair students. Give each twosome a list of several two-digit numbers, one copy of the mat on page 160, and a paper cup filled with popcorn. One youngster in each twosome reads the first number aloud. To represent the number, his partner sets one piece of popcorn on the mat for each ten and one. After the first student verifies his work, he clears the mat. The youngsters trade roles and continue in a like manner for the remainder of the list. Serve popcorn for a tasty conclusion!

- Look high and low, and you won't find a small-group game with more kid appeal! Label three blank cards "Highest" and three blank cards "Lowest." Place them in a bag. Give each student a copy of the mat on page 160 and a number of small manipulatives. At your signal, each student places the manipulatives on her mat to represent a number of her choice. Draw a card and read it aloud. The student with the type of number indicated on the card earns one point. Return the card to the bag and play a desired number of additional rounds. The player with the greatest number of points wins.

Popcorn, Anyone?

Clara the clown is selling popcorn.
How many pieces does she have in each set?
To find out, **write** how many tens and ones.
Write the number on the line.

Popcorn Key

= 1 piece

= 10 pieces

a.  | tens | ones |
|------|------|
| | |

_____

b.  | tens | ones |
|------|------|
| | |

_____

c.  | tens | ones |
|------|------|
| | |

_____

d.  | tens | ones |
|------|------|
| | |

_____

e.  | tens | ones |
|------|------|
| | |

_____

f.  | tens | ones |
|------|------|
| | |

_____

Bonus Box: Clara's friend Clancey has 25 pieces of popcorn. On the back of this sheet, use the Popcorn Key to show 25 pieces. Write the number of tens and ones.

©2001 The Education Center, Inc. • *Math Skills Workout* • TEC3225 • Key p. 167

Hooked on Place Value

Students are sure to fall for this place-value activity—hook, line, and sinker!

Purpose: To count, identify, and rewrite sets of tens and ones

Students will do the following:

- count sets of tens and ones
- group objects into sets of tens and ones
- rewrite sets of tens and ones

Materials for each student:

- copy of page 16
- pencil
- crayons

Vocabulary to review:

- set
- group
- tens
- ones

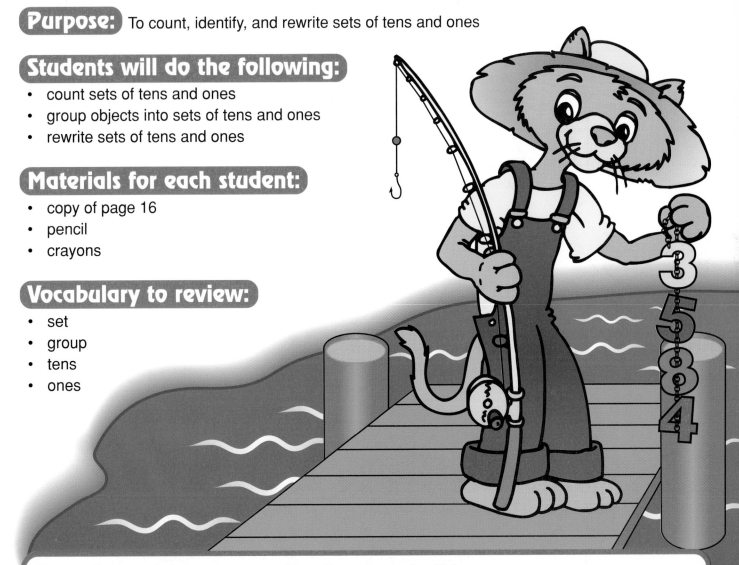

Extension activities to use after the reproducible:

- Students get the scoop on place value *and* number order with this class activity! For each student, scoop a number of dried beans onto a paper plate. The youngster groups the beans into sets of ten. He counts the number of tens and ones and records the total on a provided card. In turn, each student reports his total to the class. With your assistance, he uses a loop of tape to affix the card to the chalkboard, creating a class number line. If there are any duplicate number cards, display the like numbers in columns.

- Shake up place-value practice! Pair students and give each twosome one die. Each youngster will also need a sheet of paper and a pencil. Each student divides her paper into two columns. She labels the left column "tens" and the right column "ones." To play a round, one student rolls the die and records the number on top of the die in the tens column. She repeats the process for the ones column. Her partner takes a turn in a like manner. The player who has the greater number earns one point. Play continues for a desired number of rounds. The player with the higher score wins.

Hooked on Place Value

For each set of fish, **circle** each group of ten.
Write how many tens and ones. **Write** the number.
Color the fish and the matching cat the same color.

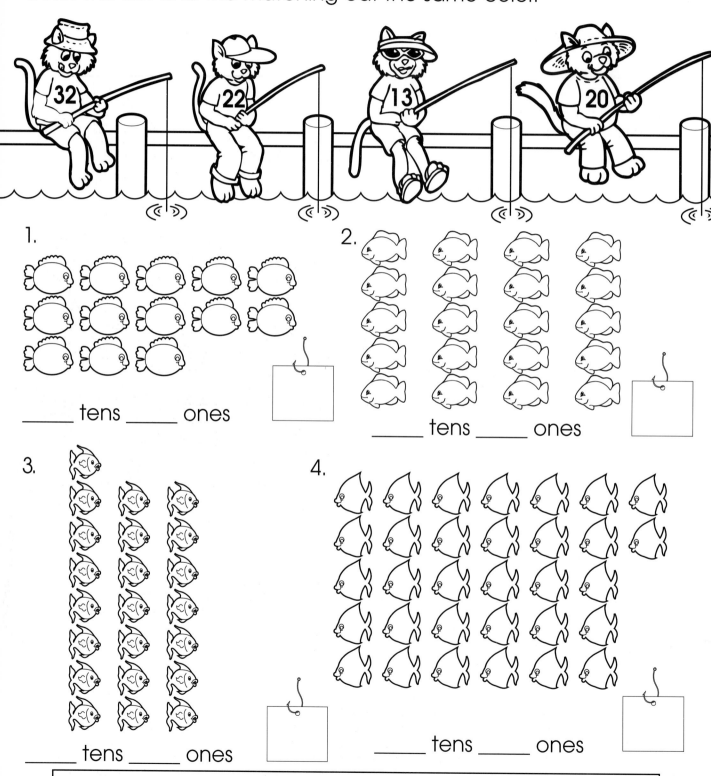

1.

_____ tens _____ ones

2.

_____ tens _____ ones

3.

_____ tens _____ ones

4.

_____ tens _____ ones

Bonus Box: On the back of this sheet, draw a set of fish that has seven more fish than set 1. Color each set of ten a different color. Write the number of fish in all.

It's Show Time!

Now presenting a beginning addition activity that's bound to be a hands-down favorite!

Purpose: To understand the concept of addition

Students will do the following:

- count sets of pictured objects to determine the sum
- draw sets of objects to represent an addition sentence

Materials for each student:

- copy of page 18
- pencil
- purple crayon
- black crayon

Vocabulary to review:

- in all
- sum
- addition sentence

5 + 4 = 9

Extension activities to use after the reproducible:

- Here's a handy way to help students grasp the concept of addition! Pair students. Give each student a 9" x 12" sheet of white paper, crayons, and ten cubes. Each youngster traces his hands on the paper (with his partner's help as needed). He places one or more cubes in each of his drawn hands and writes the corresponding addition sentence. Next, the student removes the cubes from his paper. He challenges his partner to read the addition sentence aloud and place the corresponding numbers of cubes on the hands. After the youngster verifies his partner's work, the students switch roles.

- Hatch addition facts through 12 with this "egg-cellent" center! Put 24 Unifix® cubes—12 of one color and 12 of another—in a basket. Program a sheet of paper with addition sentence frames like the following: ____ + ____ = ____. Make a number of copies. Place the copies, the basket, and an egg carton in a center stocked with pencils. A student places one cube in each egg carton section. Then she writes the number of each color cube in the first two blanks of the first sentence frame. After she writes the sum, the student returns the cubes to the basket, refills the egg carton with a different color combination of cubes, and continues in a like manner to complete the sheet.

It's Show Time!

The handy math magician has
   some tricks up his sleeve!
How many cubes does he make
   appear?

Write the number in all.

1.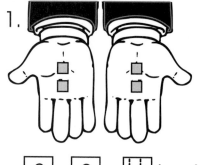

$\boxed{2} + \boxed{2} = \boxed{4}$ in all

2.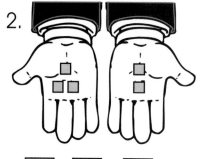

$\boxed{3} + \boxed{2} = \boxed{}$ in all

1 + 1 = 2

Write the sum.

3.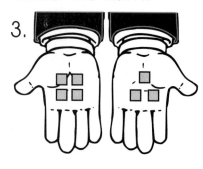

4 + 3 = _____

4.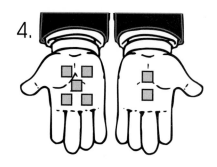

5 + 2 = _____

5.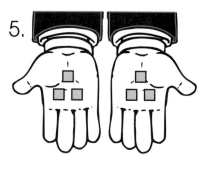

3 + 3 = _____

Draw. Write the sum.

6.

1 + 3 = _____

7.

2 + 4 = _____

8.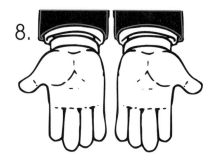

4 + 1 = _____

Bonus Box: On the back of this sheet, draw a magic hat that has 3 purple stripes and 3
black stripes. Write an addition sentence to match.

All Aboard!

Here's a reproducible activity specially engineered to get your students on track with addition!

Purpose: To understand the concept of addition

Students will do the following:

- match pictured sets with addition sentences

Materials for each student:

- copy of page 20
- scissors
- glue
- pencil
- green crayon
- brown crayon

Vocabulary to review:

- plus
- equals
- sum

Extension activities to use after the reproducible:

- What's down on the farm? Plenty of addition reinforcement! Each youngster illustrates her favorite barnyard critter on a four-inch white construction paper square. Then she tapes a jumbo craft stick to the back of it to create a stick puppet. Invite several students to stand at the front of the room with their puppets and group themselves by type of animal. Then ask a volunteer to tell an addition story about the animals, such as "four pigs sitting and two cows eating make six animals in all." Have other groups of students represent similar addition stories until every youngster has had a turn with her puppet.

- This partner center serves up number-sentence practice by the cupful! Randomly place one to ten counters in each of 12 paper cups. Code the cups to make two sets of six. Place each set on a different Styrofoam® tray (or in a box lid) for easy storage. Place the prepared cups in a center stocked with paper and pencils. When a twosome visits the center, each student selects a different set of cups. Each youngster, in turn, counts the contents of one cup and reports the total to his partner. Then the students write an addition sentence that reflects their combined total. The youngsters continue with the remaining cups in a like manner.

20 Name _____

All Aboard!

Cut on the dotted lines.
Put a drop of glue on each •.
Glue on the matching train car.

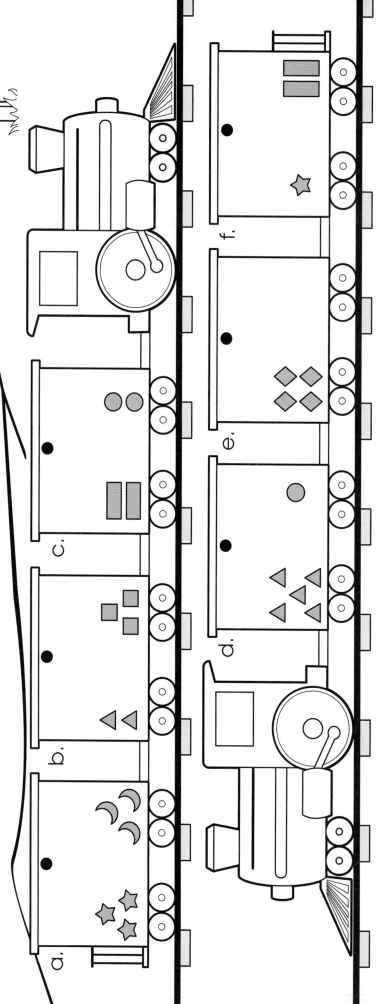

Next Stop:
Sum Town

Bonus Box: On the back of this sheet, draw a picture to show a train with 4 green cars and 4 brown cars. Write an addition sentence to match.

| 2 + 3 = 5 | 4 + 0 = 4 | 1 + 2 = 3 | 3 + 3 = 6 | 5 + 1 = 6 | 2 + 2 = 4 |

Mission Addition

Blast off into a galaxy of addition fun with problems in a horizontal format!

Purpose: To solve horizontal addition problems

Students will do the following:

- use pictures to solve horizontal addition problems
- draw pictures to solve horizontal addition problems
- solve horizontal addition problems with sums to 10

Materials for each student:

- copy of page 22
- pencil
- 12 counters
- crayons

Vocabulary to review:

- addition
- sum
- number sentence
- solve
- problem

$6 + 2 = \underline{8}$

Extension activities to use after the reproducible:

- Get the story on horizontal addition with this class display! Cut a number of sentence strips in half to make a class supply. Program each strip with a different addition sentence. Give each student a strip and a sheet of drawing paper. Have the youngster draw a picture to correspond with the addition sentence. Then letter the pictures for easy reference and display them below the title "What's the Addition Story?" Invite each youngster to read his addition sentence aloud and challenge his classmates to identify the corresponding picture. Ask the youngster who identifies it to tell the pictured addition story. (For example, "The baker sells three cakes and six cookies. He sells nine desserts in all.") Then post each strip near its picture.

- What's the perfect visual aid for writing number sentences? Why, dominoes, of course! Place a number of selected dominoes in a container. For independent practice, a student divides a sheet of math paper into quarters. She removes one domino from the container and sets it horizontally on her work surface. In one section of the math paper, the youngster writes an addition sentence that represents the domino dots. Then she turns the domino so that it is vertical and writes the corresponding vertical addition sentence in the same section of the paper. The student repeats the process with different dominoes until she has written two number sentences in each section.

Mission Addition

Count the spaceships.
Write the sums.

1. ⬣ + ⬣ = ____   2. ⬣ + ⬣ = ____

3. ⬣ + ⬣ = ____   4. ⬣ + ⬣ = ____

Draw spaceships.
Write the sums.

5. [ ] + [ ] = ____
   3   3

6. [ ] + [ ] = ____
   2   3

Solve the problems.
Use counters if needed.
Write the sums.

7. 6 + 3 = ____   8. 8 + 0 = ____   9. 5 + 5 = ____

10. 3 + 3 = ____   11. 2 + 5 = ____   12. 1 + 8 = ____

Bonus Box: Marty Martian finds 3 space rocks. Ally Alien finds 7 space rocks. How many space rocks do they find in all? On the back of this sheet, write a number sentence to show the answer. Draw a picture to go with it.

Mitten Mania

Warm up students' addition skills with this handy reproducible!

Purpose: To solve addition problems in a vertical format

Students will do the following:

• solve addition problems with sums to 10

Materials for each student:

• copy of page 24
• pencil
• crayons

Vocabulary to review:

• add
• sum
• odd
• even

Extension activities to use after the reproducible:

• These snow pals are dressed for winter *and* addition practice! For each student, program a blank card with an unsolved vertical addition problem. Give each student a prepared card, three five-inch white paper circles, one 6" x 9" piece of construction paper, and one 12" x 18" sheet of construction paper. To make a snow pal, the youngster uses crayons to draw a face on one circle. For each addend, he draws a corresponding number of buttons on a different circle. The youngster assembles and glues the snow pal on the large sheet of paper. He uses the small piece of paper to make a hat cutout. Then he labels it with the corresponding addition fact and glues it on the snow pal. Display your students' completed snow pals below the title "Frosty Facts."

• Build students' addition skills with this hands-on activity! Divide students into small groups. Give each group crayons, a sheet of paper, ten Unifix® cubes of one color, and ten cubes of another color. Ask the students in each group to use ten cubes to build a tower. Have them write and illustrate the corresponding vertical addition sentence. (If the tower is only one color, instruct the youngsters to use a 0 to represent the second color in the number sentence.) Challenge the youngsters to represent and record all of the remaining combinations for sums of 10.

Mitten Mania

Oh no! Katie Kitten has lost her mittens!
To find them, **write** the sums.
Look for the mittens that have a sum of 10.
Label them "K" for Katie.

$$\begin{array}{r} 5 \\ +3 \\ \hline \end{array}$$ d.

$$\begin{array}{r} 8 \\ +1 \\ \hline \end{array}$$ a.

$$\begin{array}{r} 7 \\ +0 \\ \hline \end{array}$$ c.

$$\begin{array}{r} 6 \\ +4 \\ \hline \end{array}$$ b.

$$\begin{array}{r} 3 \\ +3 \\ \hline \end{array}$$ h.

$$\begin{array}{r} 5 \\ +2 \\ \hline \end{array}$$ e.

$$\begin{array}{r} 1 \\ +9 \\ \hline \end{array}$$ g.

$$\begin{array}{r} 2 \\ +7 \\ \hline \end{array}$$ f.

$$\begin{array}{r} 4 \\ +2 \\ \hline \end{array}$$ i.

$$\begin{array}{r} 5 \\ +4 \\ \hline \end{array}$$ j.

Bonus Box: Use a green crayon to outline each mitten that has an even sum.
Use a purple crayon to outline each mitten that has an odd sum.

Flavorful Facts

Scoop up a hearty helping of addition practice with this cool activity!

Purpose: To solve addition problems in a vertical format

Students will do the following:

- solve addition problems with sums to 12

Materials for each student:

- copy of page 26
- pencil
- brown crayon

Vocabulary to review:

- add
- sum

Extension activities to use after the reproducible:

- Here's a totally terrific addition center! Program each of ten blank cards with vertical addition problems and write the corresponding sum on the back of each one. For each problem, use adhesive dots to represent the addends on an unprogrammed card. (See the pictured example.) After you prepare a dot card for each problem card, shuffle all of the cards and place them in a decorated envelope in a center. When a student visits the center, he pairs each problem card with the correct dot card. He mentally solves the problem (with the use of the dots, if necessary), then flips the problem card to check his answer.

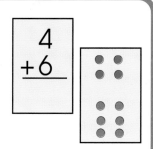

- Showcase students' vertical addition skills with these colorful booklets! Give each student ten two-inch construction paper squares. Also provide her with a five-page 6" x 12" booklet that has been stapled along a short end. To complete the booklet, she places it on her desk so that the staples are at the top. She labels each square with a number from 1 to 10. On each booklet page, the youngster glues two squares to represent the addends of a vertical problem. She finishes setting up the problem and then writes the sum. After the youngster personalizes the booklet cover, encourage her to take her one-of-a-kind collection of facts home to share with her family.

Flavorful Facts

Clyde Cow is dreaming up some new flavors!
Write the sum on each cone.
Use a brown crayon to outline the ice-cream treats that have
    sums of 12.

a.
$$\begin{array}{r} 8 \\ + 2 \\ \hline 10 \end{array}$$

b.
$$\begin{array}{r} 1 \\ + 11 \\ \hline \end{array}$$

g.
$$\begin{array}{r} 2 \\ + 10 \\ \hline \end{array}$$

c.
$$\begin{array}{r} 5 \\ + 6 \\ \hline \end{array}$$

d.
$$\begin{array}{r} 4 \\ + 5 \\ \hline \end{array}$$

f.
$$\begin{array}{r} 6 \\ + 6 \\ \hline \end{array}$$

h.
$$\begin{array}{r} 3 \\ + 7 \\ \hline \end{array}$$

e.
$$\begin{array}{r} 7 \\ + 4 \\ \hline \end{array}$$

i.
$$\begin{array}{r} 9 \\ + 3 \\ \hline \end{array}$$

Bonus Box: If Clyde sells 2 ice-cream treats on Saturday and 9 treats on Sunday, how many treats does he sell in all? On the back of this sheet, write and illustrate a number sentence to show the answer.

Buggy Over Doubles!

Spotting doubles is sure to be a snap with these friendly beetles!

Purpose: To use doubles to find sums

Students will do the following:

- use pictures to complete doubles facts through 12
- draw pictures to complete doubles facts through 12
- use doubles to find sums through 12

Materials for each student:

- copy of page 28
- pencil
- crayons
- die

Vocabulary to review:

- double
- fact

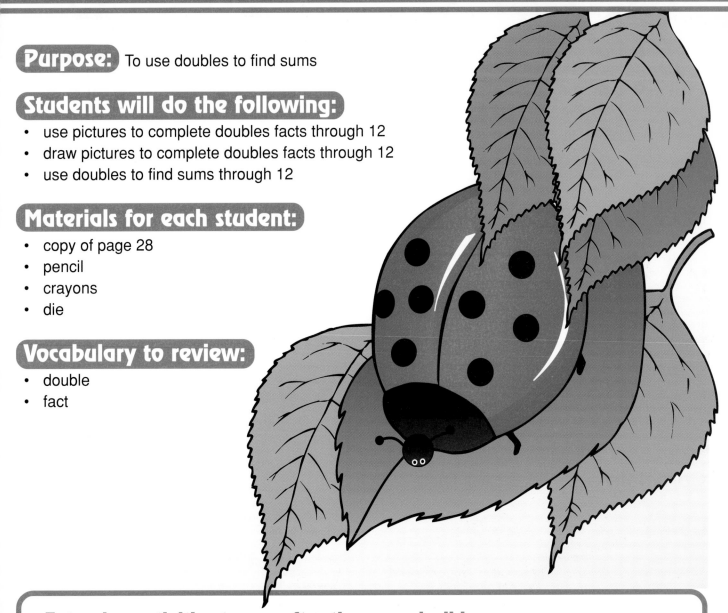

Extension activities to use after the reproducible:

- This doubles center gets two thumbs-ups! Place a class supply of 9" x 12" construction paper, a set of flash cards numbered 2–6, pencils, wet wipes, and a shallow dish of paint in a center. A student folds her paper in half, unfolds it, and then lays it flat. She selects a number card, dips her thumb into the paint, and makes the corresponding number of thumbprints on one half of the paper. Immediately afterward, the student refolds the paper, presses it lightly, and unfolds it. She then writes the corresponding doubles fact below the prints.

- Here's a unique activity that doubles math fun! For each twosome, provide a mirror, six cubes, a die, pencils, and two sheets of paper. One student holds the mirror upright on a desk. His partner rolls the die and reads the top number. He places the corresponding number of cubes in front of the mirror and then counts them, including the cubes in the reflection. After each student writes the corresponding doubles fact on his paper, the partners trade roles. They repeat the activity as time allows.

Buggy Over Doubles!

Count the spots. **Complete** each doubles fact.

 a.

 b.

 c.

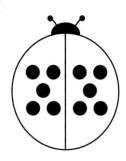 d.

2 + 2 = _____   4 + 4 = _____   3 + 3 = _____   5 + 5 = _____

Color the spots. **Complete** each doubles fact.

 e.

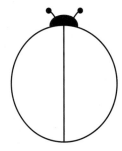 f.

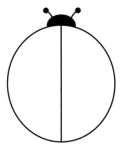 g.

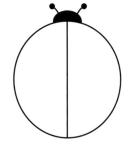 h.

1 + 1 = _____   3 + 3 = _____   6 + 6 = _____   2 + 2 = _____

Complete each doubles fact.

i. 5 + 5 = _____   j. 2 + 2 = _____   k. 1 + 1 = _____   l. 3 + 3 = _____

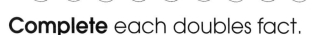

Complete each doubles fact.

m.
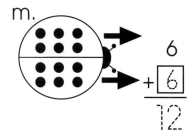
6
+ 6
12

n.
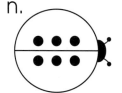

3
+ ☐

o.
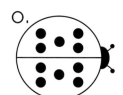

☐
+ ☐

 **Bonus Box:** Roll a die. On the back of this sheet, write the number rolled. Use the number to write a doubles fact. Draw and color a picture to match.

All in the Family

Use this neighborly collection of problems to help students feel right at home with fact families!

Purpose: To complete fact families

Students will do the following:
- solve addition and subtraction problems
- complete addition and subtraction facts
- identify the numbers in a fact family

Materials for each student:
- copy of page 30
- pencil

Vocabulary to review:
- fact
- fact family

Extension activities to use after the reproducible:

- There's no place like these fact family homes! Give each student a 9" x 12" sheet of construction paper. Help the youngster place a 6" x 9" piece of construction paper atop a stack of three half sheets of white paper; then staple the entire stack onto the full sheet of paper as shown. Instruct the youngster to cut away the top of the resulting booklet to resemble a house roof. Have him label each page with an assigned family of numbers, write the corresponding addition and subtraction sentences, and then personalize the cover as desired. Now that's a handy (and homey!) fact family reference!

- Shake up fact family practice with this hands-on activity! For each student, place 12 two-sided counters in a paper lunch bag. Distribute the bags and give each youngster a sheet of paper. The student shakes her bag and then spills the counters onto her desk. She sorts the counters into two sets by color. At the top of her paper, the youngster colors a picture to show each set. Then she writes the fact family for the number of counters in each set and the total. For additional practice, the youngster returns the counters to her bag, turns her paper over, and repeats the process.

All in the Family

The Fact Families are moving in!
To help them, **complete** each fact.

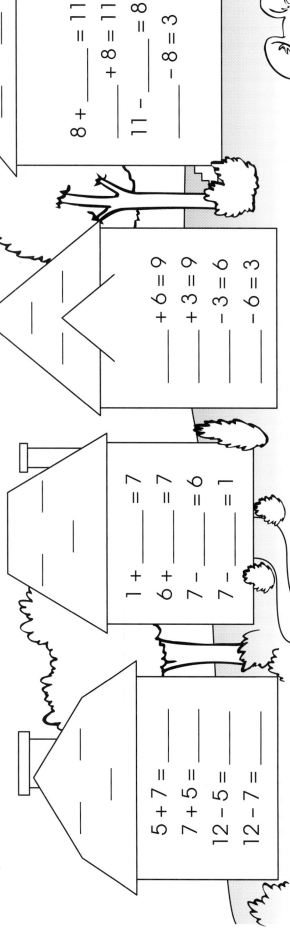

$8 + \underline{\hspace{1cm}} = 11$
$\underline{\hspace{1cm}} + 8 = 11$
$11 - \underline{\hspace{1cm}} = 8$
$\underline{\hspace{1cm}} - 8 = 3$

$\underline{\hspace{1cm}} + 6 = 9$
$\underline{\hspace{1cm}} + 3 = 9$
$\underline{\hspace{1cm}} - 3 = 6$
$\underline{\hspace{1cm}} - 6 = 3$

$1 + \underline{\hspace{1cm}} = 7$
$6 + \underline{\hspace{1cm}} = 7$
$7 - \underline{\hspace{1cm}} = 6$
$7 - \underline{\hspace{1cm}} = 1$

$5 + 7 = \underline{\hspace{1cm}}$
$7 + 5 = \underline{\hspace{1cm}}$
$12 - 5 = \underline{\hspace{1cm}}$
$12 - 7 = \underline{\hspace{1cm}}$

Now **help** Moe Mover. **Look** at each box of numbers.
Write the numbers on the roof with the matching fact family.

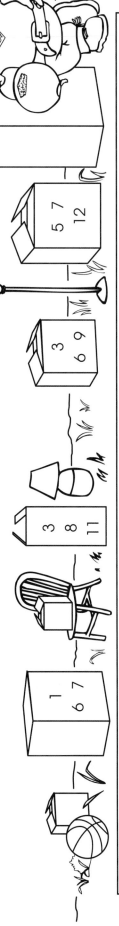

| 5 7 |
| 12 |

| 3 |
| 6 9 |

| 3 |
| 8 |
| 11 |

| 1 |
| 6 7 |

Bonus Box: Moe Mover forgot a box! It has these numbers: 4, 6, 10. On the back of this sheet, draw a large house. Write the numbers on the roof. Write the fact family on the house.

It's a Triple Play!

Strengthen addition skills with this all-star lineup of problems with three addends!

Purpose: To solve addition problems with three addends

Students will do the following:

- use manipulatives to solve addition problems
- find the sum of three addends

Materials for each student:

- copy of page 32
- pencil
- scissors

Vocabulary to review:

- add
- sum
- number sentence

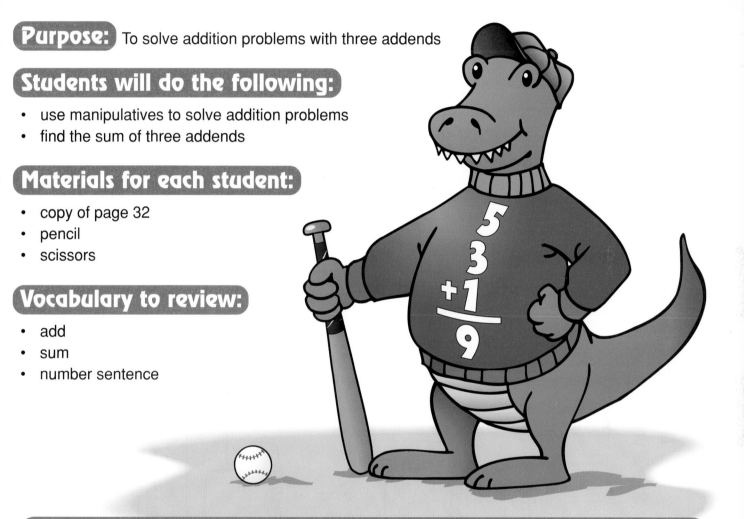

Extension activities to use after the reproducible:

- Strengthen understanding of addition with the number shuffle! Program two blank cards for each of the numbers 0 through 9. Choose three cards that total 12 or less. Have three volunteers stand at the front of the room and then give each of them a selected card to show the class. Pair two cardholders by asking them to stand together. Help the seated classmates add the paired numbers and then add the sum to the third number. Next, have the cardholders rearrange themselves to make a different pair. Help the class use the established process to determine the total. Point out that even though the numbers are in a different order, the total is the same. Provide further addition practice with different volunteers and cards.

- What's in the cards? A partner center that sharpens calculator *and* mental addition skills! Program three blank cards for each of the numbers 0 through 4. Place the cards and a calculator in a center. One student in a twosome shuffles the cards and stacks them facedown. The second student draws two cards, reads them aloud, and then announces the sum. He draws a third card and adds it to the sum. Next, the first student uses a calculator to check his partner's total. After he places the cards in a discard pile, the students trade roles. The youngsters continue taking turns (reshuffling the discarded cards as necessary) as time allows.

It's a Triple Play!

Help Coach Crocodile number the shirts.
Cut along the dotted lines.
Use the baseballs to find each sum.
Write the sums.

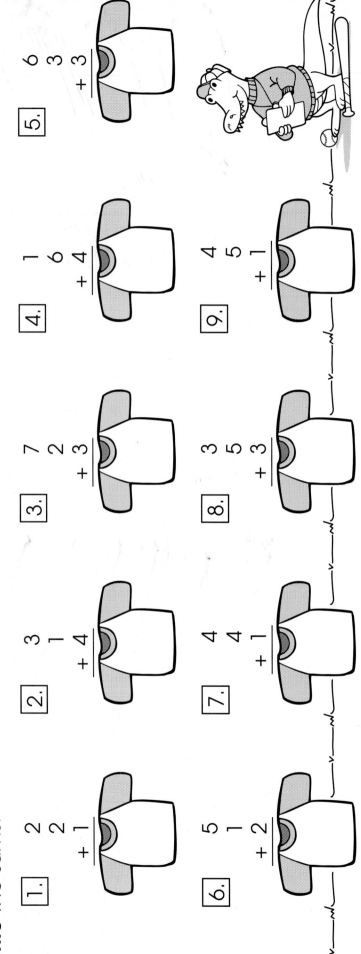

1.
```
   2
   2
 + 1
```

2.
```
   3
   1
 + 4
```

3.
```
   7
   2
 + 3
```

4.
```
   1
   6
 + 4
```

5.
```
   6
   3
 + 3
```

6.
```
   5
   1
 + 2
```

7.
```
   4
   4
 + 1
```

8.
```
   3
   5
 + 3
```

9.
```
   4
   5
 + 1
```

Bonus Box: There are 8 baseballs on the ground, 2 baseballs in the school, and 1 baseball on the bus. On the back of this sheet, write 2 different number sentences to show how many baseballs there are in all.

©2001 The Education Center, Inc. • *Math Skills Workout* • TEC3225 • Key p. 168

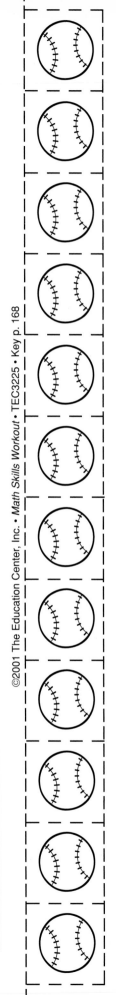

Subtraction Snapshots

Purpose: To understand the concept of subtraction

Students will do the following:

- draw pictures to represent subtraction problems
- use pictures to solve subtraction problems

Materials for each student:

- copy of page 34
- pencil
- crayons

Vocabulary to review:

- subtract
- difference
- addition sentence
- subtraction sentence

Extension activities to use after the reproducible:

- Lights, camera, subtraction! Divide students into small groups and give each group a piece of scrap paper. In each group, the youngsters write a subtraction sentence that has a minuend equal to the number of group members. Then they plan a brief skit that illustrates the subtraction sentence. The students present the skit to the class and challenge their classmates to identify the subtraction sentence. The student who correctly identifies it records it on the chalkboard. If no one correctly identifies the sentence after three guesses, a group member writes it on the board. Now that's a nifty way to bring the concept of subtraction to life!

- Draw your students into subtraction with this self-checking center! Program a class supply of blank cards with subtraction sentences. Give each student one card and a 9" x 12" sheet of white construction paper. Instruct him to place the paper on his desk horizontally and then draw a line across the paper, three inches from the bottom. Have the youngster color an illustration above the line to represent the subtraction sentence. (For example, a clown holding three balloons as two balloons float away might represent $5 - 2 = 3$.) Ask him to write the subtraction sentence on the back of the illustration. Laminate students' work; then place it in a center. When a student visits the center, he chooses an illustration, uses a wipe-off marker to write the subtraction sentence below the line, and then flips the paper to check his work.

Name _____

34

Subtraction Snapshots

Help Fran develop her snapshots!
Use your crayons to draw.
Subtract.

3. Draw 6 ⚬s.
   Draw an X on 4 of them.

   6 – 4 = _____

2. Draw 4 🍒s.
   Draw an X on 3 of them.

   4 – 3 = _____

5. Draw 7 🏀s.
   Draw an X on 5 of them.

   7 – 5 = _____

4. Draw 3 🌳s.
   Draw an X on 3 of them.

   3 – 3 = _____

1. Draw 5 ☀s.
   Draw an X on 2 of them.

   5 – 2 = _____

Bonus Box: Look at the subtraction sentence for number 1. On the back of this sheet, use the same numbers to write an addition sentence. Draw a picture to match your work.

Barrels of Subtraction Fun

Swing into subtraction with this "a-peeling" reproducible activity!

Purpose: To understand the concept of subtraction

Students will do the following:

- label pictures to represent subtraction problems
- use pictures to complete subtraction sentences

Materials for each student:

- copy of page 36
- pencil
- crayons

Vocabulary to review:

- minus
- equals
- subtraction sentence

7 - 3 = 4

Extension activities to use after the reproducible:

- Here's a unique spin on subtraction sentence practice! For every two students, label one card for each of the numerals 3–10. Divide a tagboard circle into quarters to make a spinner. Number the quarters 0–3. Use a paper clip and pencil to demonstrate how to use the spinner. Pair students and give each twosome a spinner, a sheet of paper, and a set of cards. To complete the activity, one youngster in each twosome stacks the cards facedown. She draws a card to represent a minuend. Her partner spins the spinner to determine the number to subtract. With her partner's help, she writes and solves the corresponding subtraction problem. The youngsters trade roles and continue until they have used every card.

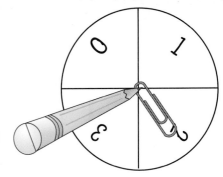

- This center activity can be prepared in a jiffy! Place a supply of sentence strips, one or more small rubber stamps, an ink pad, crayons, and two dice in a center. Title a nearby display area "Subtraction Sentence Stampede." To use the center, a student folds a strip in half and then unfolds it. He rolls the dice and then makes the corresponding number of stamps on the left-hand side of the strip. Next, the youngster rolls one die. He uses a crayon to cross out the corresponding number of stamps. On the right-hand half of the strip, he writes the subtraction sentence that is represented. Then he adds his completed strip to the display.

Name _____

Barrels of Subtraction Fun

Read. Write how many.
Complete each number sentence.
Color.

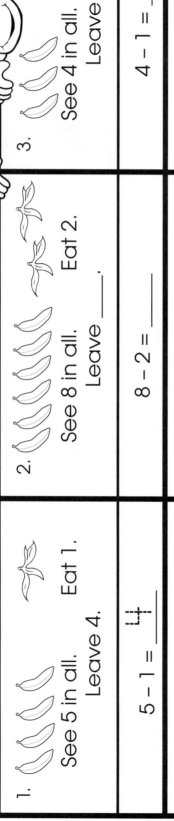

1. See 5 in all.   Eat 1.
   Leave 4.

   $5 - 1 =$ 4

2. See 8 in all.   Eat 2.
   Leave ____.

   $8 - 2 =$ ____

3. See 4 in all.   Eat 1.
   Leave ____.

   $4 - 1 =$ ____

4. See 7 in all.   Eat 2.
   Leave ____.

   $7 - 2 =$ ____

5. See 6 in all.   Eat 0.
   Leave ____.

   $6 - 0 =$ ____

6. See 7 in all.   Eat 3.
   Leave ____.

   $7 - ___ = ___$

7. See 6 in all.   Eat 1.
   Leave ____.

   $6 - ___ = ___$

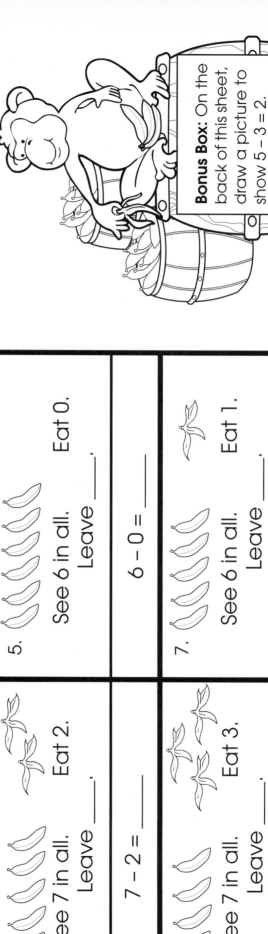

Bonus Box: On the back of this sheet, draw a picture to show 5 – 3 = 2. Write a sentence that tells about it.

©2001 The Education Center, Inc. • *Math Skills Workout* • TEC3225 • Key p. 168

Bounce Backward!

Purpose: To subtract by counting back

Students will do the following:

- count back on a number line
- count back to solve subtraction problems

Materials for each student:

- copy of page 38
- pencil

Vocabulary to review:

- subtraction
- count back
- number line
- difference

Extension activities to use after the reproducible:

- Students mentally bounce backward on a number line with this quick and easy review. Program a supply of cards with subtraction problems that use the numerals 1–10. Draw a number line labeled with the numerals 0–10 on the board. Hold up one card and have students visualize bouncing backward on the number line to solve the problem. Invite a volunteer to state the difference. Continue with a desired number of problems. When students become proficient with the activity, eliminate the number line. Follow the bouncing ball!

- Round up plenty of practice counting backward! Program a craft stick for each of the numbers 1–10. Stand the prepared sticks number side down in a cup. Have students stand in a large circle. To begin a round of play, a student volunteer removes a stick from the cup and says the number aloud. The student on her left says the preceding number. Students continue the backward count around the circle until a student says zero. The student who says zero sits down in her place. The next student in the circle then removes a numbered stick, and play continues for a desired number of rounds or until only one student remains. Count on this activity to make math fun!

Bounce Backward!

Use the number line.
Count back to find each difference.

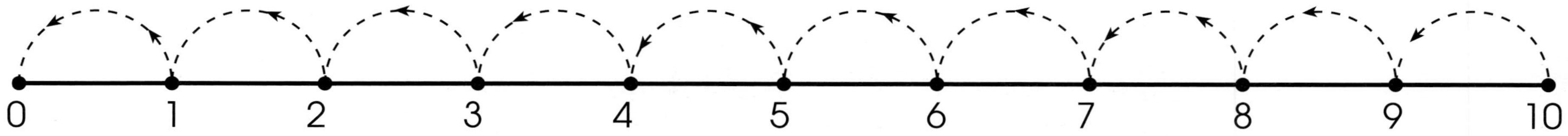

0 1 2 3 4 5 6 7 8 9 10

① $\begin{array}{r}10\\-2\\\hline\end{array}$ ⊙⊙

② $\begin{array}{r}6\\-2\\\hline\end{array}$

③ $\begin{array}{r}5\\-1\\\hline\end{array}$

④ $\begin{array}{r}4\\-2\\\hline\end{array}$

⑤ $\begin{array}{r}8\\-2\\\hline\end{array}$

⑥ $\begin{array}{r}6\\-1\\\hline\end{array}$

⑦ $\begin{array}{r}7\\-2\\\hline\end{array}$

⑧ $\begin{array}{r}2\\-1\\\hline\end{array}$

⑨ 10 – 1 = ____

⑩ 4 – 2 = ____

⑪ 9 – 3 = ____

⑫ 3 – 2 = ____

⑬ 9 – 2 = ____

⑭ 8 – 1 = ____

⑮ 5 – 3 = ____

⑯ 7 – 1 = ____

⑰ 10 – 2 = ____

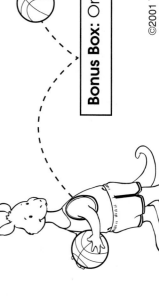

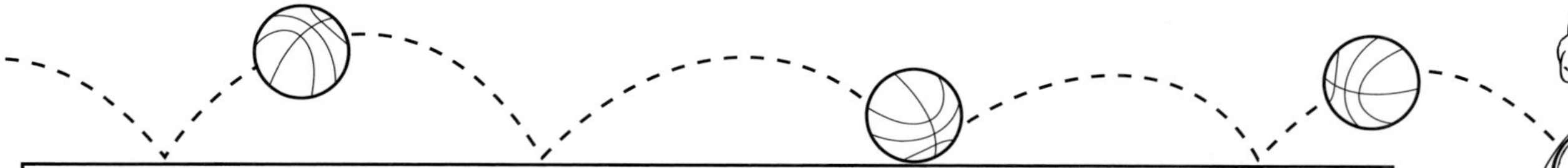

Bonus Box: On the back of this sheet, write the numbers from 20 to 0.

©2001 The Education Center, Inc. • *Math Skills Workout* • TEC3225 • Key p. 168

Have a Ball With Subtraction!

Bring subtraction skills into play with this sporty activity!

Purpose: To solve subtraction problems in a horizontal format

Students will do the following:

- complete subtraction facts through 10
- use a code

Materials for each student:

- copy of page 40
- pencil

Vocabulary to review:

- subtract
- difference

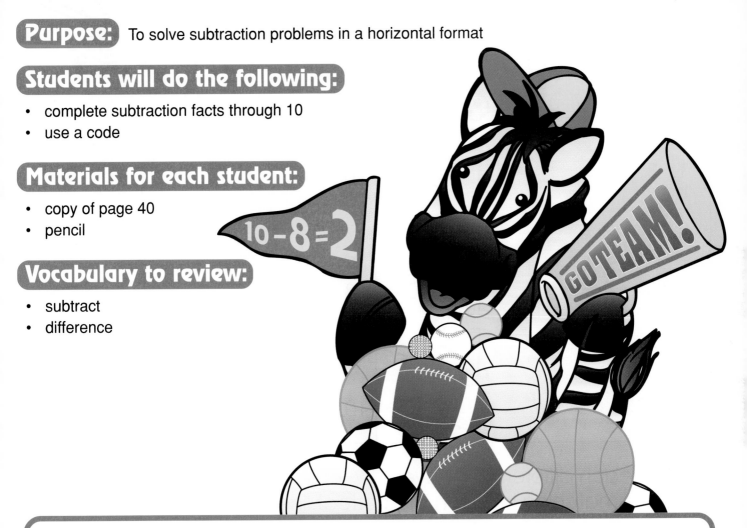

Extension activities to use after the reproducible:

- Leap into subtraction practice! Give each student a construction paper log cutout and a copy of the frog counters on page 161. Have her color and cut out the frogs. Then verbally provide a subtraction story with ten or fewer frogs, such as "Ten frogs rest on a log. Three of them go for a swim." Guide each student in using the manipulatives to act out the story and determine the difference. With students' input, record the corresponding subtraction sentence on the board. Continue with a desired number of subtraction stories. Then ask each youngster to glue the manipulatives on a 9" x 12" sheet of paper to represent her favorite story and to label it with the appropriate subtraction sentence.

- Students are sure to flip over this handy subtraction idea! Cut a sentence strip in half and put one half aside. Program the remaining half: "9 – _____ = _____." Cut 18 tagboard cards, each sized to cover a blank. Program one half of the cards with the numerals 0–9. Stack the cards and then use a metal ring to attach them to the strip above the first blank. Repeat the process for the second blank. Place the strip and a supply of manipulative in a center. To use the strip, a student flips the first stack of cards to a desired number and then flips the last stack to the correct difference. He uses the manipulatives to check his work. The youngster creates and solves additional problems as time allows.

Name _____

Have a Ball With Subtraction!

Zippy loves sports!
What sport does he like the most?
To find out, **subtract.**
Then **follow** the directions below.

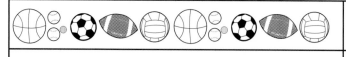 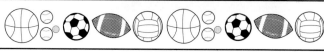

1. 3 – 0 = ____   **c**

2. 8 – 2 = ____   **k**

3. 6 – 4 = ____   **s**

4. 8 – 3 = ____   **c**

5. 10 – 0 = ____   **e**

6. 7 – 3 = ____   **o**

7. 9 – 1 = ____   **r**

8. 10 – 3 = ____   **c**

9. 3 – 2 = ____   **i**

10. 5 – 5 = ____   **k**

Look at each difference above.
Write the matching letter on the correct line.

Zippy likes ___ ___ ___ ___ ___ ___ the most because he gets a
      2   4   3   5   10   8

___ ___ ___ ___ out of it!
  6   1   7   0

Bonus Box: Zippy's favorite team played 10 games. They won 8 of them. How many games did they lose? Write a subtraction sentence on the back of this sheet to show the answer.

Soar With Subtraction!

Get ready for subtraction skills to take off with this high-flying practice!

Purpose: To solve subtraction problems in a vertical format

Students will do the following:

- complete subtraction facts through 10
- determine if subtraction problems have the same difference

Materials for each student:

- copy of page 42
- pencil
- blue crayon
- black crayon

Vocabulary to review:

- subtract
- difference
- same

Extension activities to use after the reproducible:

- Use this follow-up to take subtraction skills to new heights! At the completion of page 42, remind students that there is usually more than one way to solve a math problem, such as counting up or using manipulatives. Ask each youngster to revisit the subtraction problems and think about the strategies he used to determine the differences. Next, divide students into small groups. Have each youngster tell his group members about the strategies he used to complete his paper. Students will become more aware of their own strategies and might learn a few in the process!

- This idea is just the ticket for helping students understand the relationship between subtraction and addition! Place a card bearing a different subtraction problem on each student's desk. Give each youngster a copy of the ticket on page 161 and have her sign her name. Then establish a flight route by which each student will move to a different desk. Have each youngster take her ticket and a pencil to a classmate's desk. Ask the youngster to copy and solve the provided subtraction problem in the first column of her paper. At your signal, instruct students to continue on the route until each student has solved five problems. After each student returns to her own desk, demonstrate how to use addition to check a subtraction problem. Then have each youngster write addition sentences in the second column of her paper to verify her work.

Soar With Subtraction!

Subtract.
Look at the differences in each cloud.
Use the color code to outline the clouds.

a. $\begin{array}{r} 10 \\ -\ 6 \\ \hline \end{array}$

b. $\begin{array}{r} 8 \\ -\ 4 \\ \hline \end{array}$

c. $\begin{array}{r} 9 \\ -\ 3 \\ \hline \end{array}$

d. $\begin{array}{r} 7 \\ -\ 5 \\ \hline \end{array}$

e. $\begin{array}{r} 6 \\ -\ 5 \\ \hline \end{array}$

f. $\begin{array}{r} 4 \\ -\ 3 \\ \hline \end{array}$

g. $\begin{array}{r} 9 \\ -\ 2 \\ \hline \end{array}$

h. $\begin{array}{r} 10 \\ -\ 7 \\ \hline \end{array}$

i. $\begin{array}{r} 8 \\ -\ 5 \\ \hline \end{array}$

j. $\begin{array}{r} 3 \\ -\ 0 \\ \hline \end{array}$

Color Code
same: blue
different: black

Bonus Box: Mr. Wing saw 4 airplanes on Monday. He saw 7 airplanes on Tuesday. How many more airplanes did he see on Tuesday? Write a subtraction sentence on the back of this sheet to show the answer.

Facts to Flip Over!

Energize subtraction practice with this creative self-checking activity!

Purpose: To solve subtraction problems in a horizontal format

Students will do the following:

- complete subtraction facts through 12
- use a key to check their work

Materials for each student:

- copy of page 44
- pencil
- scissors

Vocabulary to review:

- subtract
- difference
- subtraction sentence

9 - 3 = 6

Extension activities to use after the reproducible:

- Don't be surprised if students go dotty over subtraction after visiting this independent center! Place a supply of dominoes, paper, and pencils in a center. To use the center, a student divides a sheet of paper into four equal sections. Then she positions one domino horizontally on a work surface. The youngster illustrates the domino near the top of the first section of the paper. Below the illustration, she uses the total number of dots and the number of dots on the left half of the domino to write a horizontal subtraction problem. She solves the problem, writes her answer, and then counts the number of dots on the right half of the domino to check her work. The youngster uses different dominoes to complete the remaining sections of her paper in a like manner.

- This personalized subtraction book is sure to get rave reviews! Program a class supply of cards with horizontal subtraction problems. Give each student one card and a sheet of story paper. The youngster writes and solves the subtraction problem on the first line of the paper. Below the problem he writes a corresponding school-based subtraction story (see the pictured example). Then he illustrates his work in the provided space. Bind students' completed pages into a class book titled "Schooltime Subtraction." Now that's a kid-pleasing way to get the story on everyday math!

12 - 2 = 10
There are 12 girls in our class. Two of them are absent. That means ten girls are here today.

Name

Horizontal subtraction for facts through 12

Facts to Flip Over!

Fold on the dotted line so that the ★ does not show.
Write each difference.
Unfold the paper.

a. 6 – 2 = ☐

b. 5 – 8 = ☐

c. 11 – 3 = ☐

d. 12 – 2 = ☐

e. 10 – 6 = ☐

f. 9 – 3 = ☐

g. 12 – 10 = ☐

h. 7 – 2 = ☐

Bonus Box: At the Silly Time Circus, there are 12 elephants and 8 monkeys. How many more elephants than monkeys are there? Write a subtraction sentence on the back of this sheet to show your answer.

©2001 The Education Center, Inc. • *Math Skills Workout* • TEC3225

Now **cut** along the dotted line.
Flip this piece of paper.
Place it beside your math.
Check your work.

| 4 |
| 3 |
| 2 |
| 6 |
| 4 |
| 10 |
| 8 |
| 5 |

A Garden of Groups

When it comes to planting the seeds of understanding, this multiplication activity is the cream of the crop!

Purpose: To count equal groups to determine how many in all

Students will do the following:

- circle equal groups
- identify how many in all

Materials for each student:

- copy of page 46
- pencil
- crayons

Vocabulary to review:

- equal
- group

Extension activities to use after the reproducible:

- Here's an "eggs-traordinary" way to reinforce the concept of multiplication! Place an empty egg carton, a pair of dice, and a supply of counters in a center. Arrange for two students to visit the center at one time. One youngster in each twosome rolls the dice and announces the total number rolled. He places two counters in each of the corresponding number of egg carton sections. Then his partner counts by twos (or counts the manipulatives) to determine the total number of counters in the carton. He removes the counters. Then the partners trade roles and repeat the process as time allows.

- Build mathematical understanding with this small-group activity! Give each student in the group five Unifix® cubes. Announce a number from two to five. Instruct each student to build a tower with the corresponding number of cubes. Have the students work together to determine the total number of cubes in the group's towers. Verify the students' answer; then have them take the towers apart. Continue in a like manner with different numbers. For a whole-class challenge, have every student build a two-cube tower. Then have the students determine the total number of cubes used.

A Garden of Groups

Farmer Faye has a lot of food in her garden!
Circle, count, and **write** to find out how
much she has.

1. Circle groups of 2.

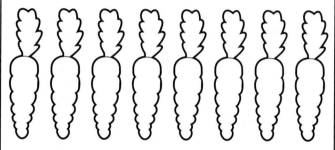

How many in all? ____

2. Circle groups of 3.

How many in all? ____

3. Circle groups of 4.

How many in all? ____

4. Circle groups of 5.

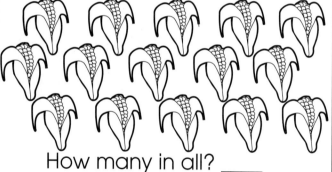

How many in all? ____

5. Circle groups of 3.

How many in all? ____

6. Circle groups of 4.

How many in all? ____

Bonus Box: On the back of this sheet, draw 4 pigs. Write how many legs they have in all.

Balloons by the Bunch

Introduce the concept of division with this festive reproducible!

Purpose: To make equal sets

Students will do the following:

- use counters to make equal sets
- draw pictures to represent equal sets
- determine how many are in each set

Materials for each student:

- copy of page 48
- pencil
- scissors

Vocabulary to review:

- equal
- sets

Extension activities to use after the reproducible:

- This hands-on division activity gives students a new way to look at numbers! Pair students. Give each twosome 12 counters, a sheet of drawing paper, and crayons. One student divides the paper in half. Then he arranges the counters to show one way to divide them into equal sets. On one half of the paper, his partner illustrates the sets and writes a description of them using the following sentence frame: "Twelve is _____ sets of _____." The students trade roles to determine a different way to divide the counters into equal sets and represent their solution on the remaining half of the paper. For more division fun, challenge students to determine all possible ways to divide the counters into equal sets.

- When it comes to reinforcing the concept of division, this center is unequaled! On each of four paper lunch bags, write a different division task using this format: "Make [number] equal sets." Determine an appropriate number of counters for the task. On the back of the bag, write how many counters should be in each set based on this number. Place the counters in the bag, then stand each prepared bag in a center. To use the center, a youngster removes the contents of one bag and follows the directions. Then she looks at the back of the bag to check her work. She returns the counters to the bag and continues with the remaining bags in a like manner.

Balloons by the Bunch

Cut on the dotted lines.
Use the balloons to make equal sets.
Draw the sets. **Complete** each sentence.

1. Use 6 balloons. Make 2 equal sets.

There are _____ balloons in each set.

2. Use 8 balloons. Make 2 equal sets.

There are _____ balloons in each set.

3. Use 4 balloons. Make 2 equal sets.

There are _____ balloons in each set.

4. Use 6 balloons. Make 3 equal sets.

There are _____ balloons in each set.

Bonus Box: On the back of this sheet, draw 10 gift boxes. Circle them to make 2 equal sets.

©2001 The Education Center, Inc. • *Math Skills Workout* • TEC3225 • Key p. 169

Fraction Flowers

Cultivate students' understanding of fractions with this colorful activity!

Purpose: To identify fractional parts of a plane figure ($\frac{1}{2}$, $\frac{1}{3}$, $\frac{1}{4}$)

Students will do the following:

- identify fractional parts of a plane figure
- use a code to classify plane figures by their fractional parts

Materials for each student:

- copy of page 50
- pencil
- crayons

Vocabulary to review:

- fraction
- halves
- thirds
- fourths

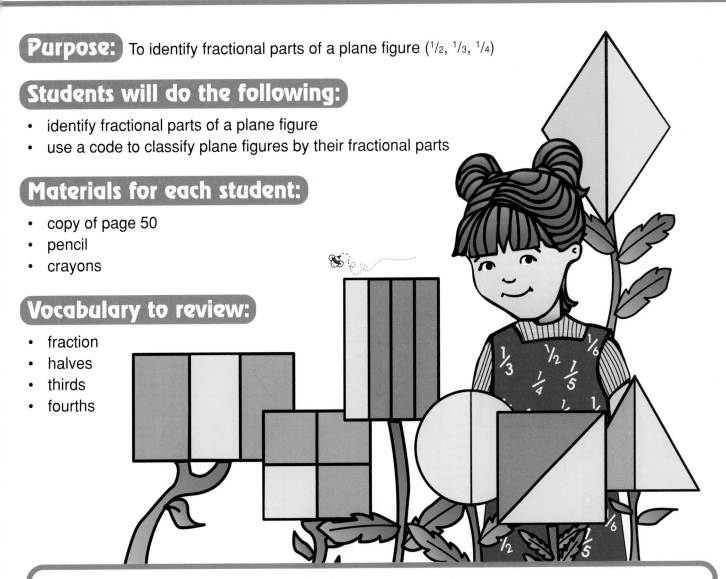

Extension activities to use after the reproducible:

- Stretch students' creativity with this fraction display! Remind students of the fraction-shaped flowers on the reproducible. Then ask them to imagine a place where everything is made of fractions! To have each student illustrate his ideas, provide access to circle, square, and equilateral triangle templates. Also provide crayons, scissors, glue, and a supply of construction paper. A student makes a desired number of shape cutouts. He uses his crayons to divide each cutout into two, three, or four equal parts. The youngster glues the cutouts in a desired arrangement on a sheet of construction paper. Then he incorporates them into an illustration. Display students' shapely pictures below the title "Welcome to Fraction Land!" to prompt discussion about fractions.

- This fraction puzzle center is sure to be a favorite! Cut out three circles, each from a different color of construction paper. Cut one into halves, one into thirds, and one into fourths. Label a blank card for each fraction represented. Color-code the back of it for self-checking. Store the materials in a decorative envelope and place the envelope at a center. A student assembles the circles, then places the corresponding fraction card beside each one. She flips the cards to check her work. For a more challenging activity, prepare like-colored puzzles.

Fraction Flowers

Mary Math has a very special garden.
All of the flowers show fractions!
Use the color code to color the flowers.

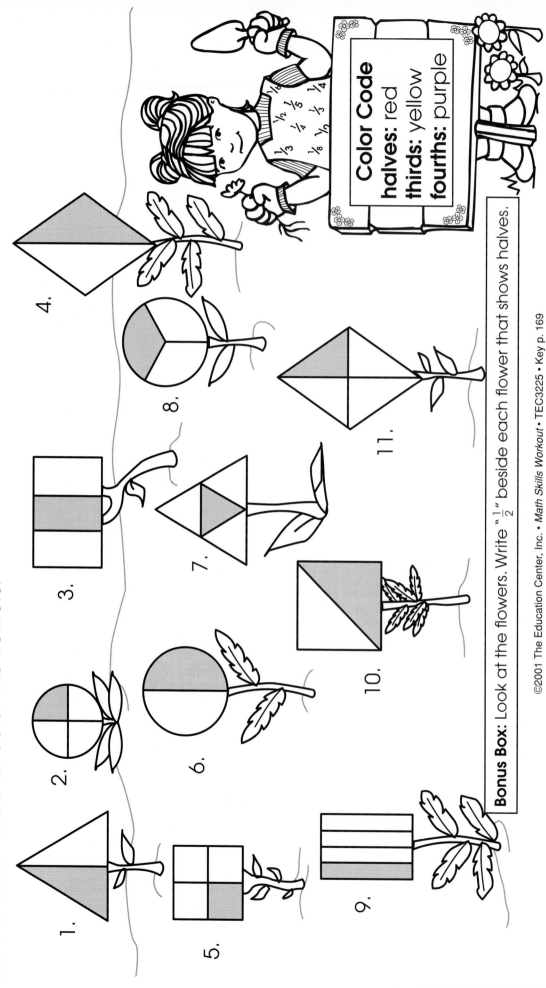

Color Code
halves: red
thirds: yellow
fourths: purple

1.

2.

3.

4.

5.

6.

7.

8.

9.

10.

11.

Bonus Box: Look at the flowers. Write "$\frac{1}{2}$" beside each flower that shows halves.

Serving Up Fractions

Give students a taste of fractions with this tantalizing reproducible!

Purpose: To identify and write fractional parts of plane figures

Students will do the following:

- identify the fractional parts of a whole ($^1/_2$, $^1/_3$, $^1/_4$)
- write fractions for parts of a whole ($^1/_2$, $^1/_3$, $^1/_4$)

Materials for each student:

- copy of page 52
- pencil
- crayons

Vocabulary to review:

- fraction
- part
- whole
- equal

Extension activities to use after the reproducible:

- Fractions are everywhere—even at meals! To demonstrate, cut a slice of bread in half. Point out that the bread is now in two equal pieces. Write the corresponding fraction ($^1/_2$) on the board. Cut the bread again to represent $^1/_4$. Then have students similarly illustrate fractions with pretend meals. To do so, give each student a paper plate, a paper square to represent a slice of bread, a paper circle for a cookie, and a paper rectangle for a carrot. The youngster folds the square twice, unfolds it, and then cuts it into quarters. She labels each piece "$^1/_4$" and glues it on the plate. The youngster uses the cookie and carrot to represent halves and thirds. Display students' fraction-filled plates on a bulletin board covered with a checkered cloth and titled "Fraction Feast." Then serve quartered peanut butter sandwiches to celebrate your students' learning success!

- Attract students to fraction practice with this center! Collect several metal pans or tin lids. Trace each pan or lid on construction paper and cut out the tracing. Then cut each cutout into a desired number of fractional pieces. Label each piece with the corresponding fraction and attach a self-adhesive magnet to the back of it. Scramble the pieces and store them in an envelope. Place the prepared materials in a center. To use the center, a student arranges the pieces on the correct pans or lids to form wholes.

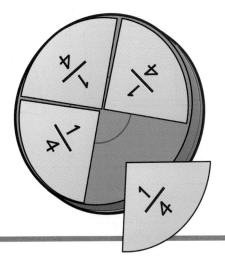

Name _____

Serving Up Fractions

Pete's Pizza Place makes pizza
   in many shapes.
Color the shaded part of each
   pizza red.
Circle the correct fraction.

1. 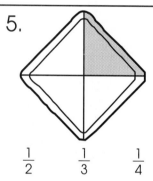 $\frac{1}{2}$ $\frac{1}{3}$ $\frac{1}{4}$	2. 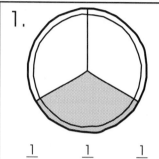 $\frac{1}{2}$ $\frac{1}{3}$ $\frac{1}{4}$	3. 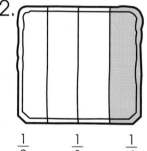 $\frac{1}{2}$ $\frac{1}{3}$ $\frac{1}{4}$	4. 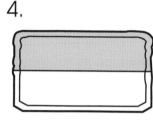 $\frac{1}{2}$ $\frac{1}{3}$ $\frac{1}{4}$

1.

$\frac{1}{2}$ $\frac{1}{3}$ $\frac{1}{4}$

2.

$\frac{1}{2}$ $\frac{1}{3}$ $\frac{1}{4}$

3.

$\frac{1}{2}$ $\frac{1}{3}$ $\frac{1}{4}$

4.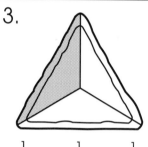

$\frac{1}{2}$ $\frac{1}{3}$ $\frac{1}{4}$

5.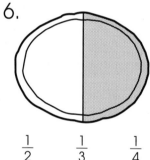

$\frac{1}{2}$ $\frac{1}{3}$ $\frac{1}{4}$

6.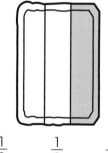

$\frac{1}{2}$ $\frac{1}{3}$ $\frac{1}{4}$

7.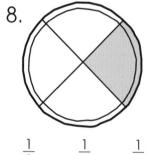

$\frac{1}{2}$ $\frac{1}{3}$ $\frac{1}{4}$

8.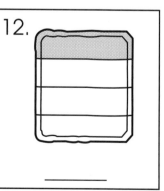

$\frac{1}{2}$ $\frac{1}{3}$ $\frac{1}{4}$

Look at the pizzas below.
Color the shaded part yellow.
Write the correct fraction.

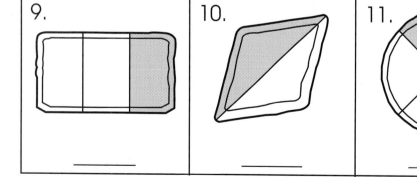

9. _____

10. _____

11. _____

12. _____

Bonus Box: On the back of this sheet, draw a large circle. Draw lines on it to divide
it into 4 equal parts. Draw a pizza topping on each part. Label each piece with the
correct fraction.

Fine-Feathered Fractions

Success with this fraction activity puts a feather in every student's cap!

Purpose: To identify fractional parts of a set ($\frac{1}{2}$, $\frac{1}{3}$, $\frac{1}{4}$)

Students will do the following:

- indicate fractional parts of sets
- identify the fraction represented by a set

Materials for each student:

- copy of page 54
- pencil
- crayons

Vocabulary to review:

- fraction
- equal
- set

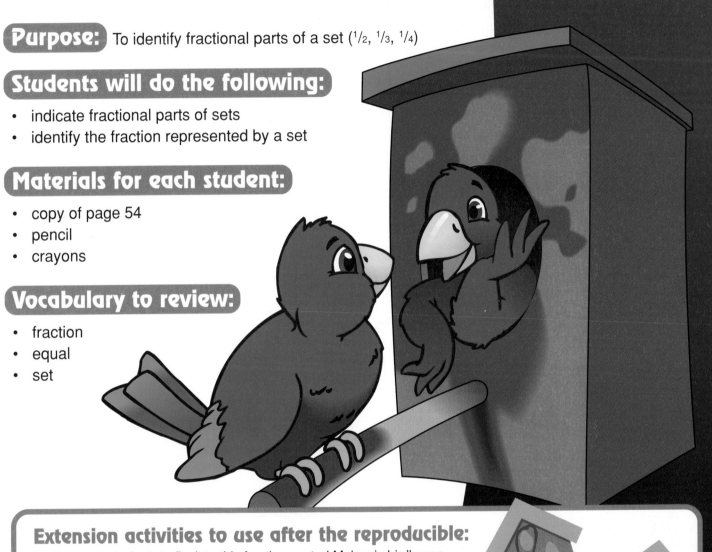

Extension activities to use after the reproducible:

- Count on students to flock to this fraction center! Make six birdhouse cutouts similar to the one shown. Label two for each of the following fractions: $\frac{1}{2}$, $\frac{1}{3}$, and $\frac{1}{4}$. Program the cutouts with two, three, or four seeds, respectively, varying the arrangement of the seeds. Letter each cutout; then laminate it. Place the cutouts, a prepared answer key, and a wipe-off marker in a center. For each cutout, a student reads the fraction and then circles the appropriate number of seeds. She uses the answer key to check her work and then wipes the cutouts clean. For a more challenging center, program the cutouts with multiples of two, three, or four seeds.

- Strengthen students' understanding of fractional parts with this class activity! Divide students into groups of three. Give each group 20 cubes, a length of yarn, and one 9" x 12" sheet of felt to use as a workmat. Announce a number from two to 20. Instruct the students in each group to place the corresponding number of cubes on the workmat. Have them divide the cubes into a specified number of equal sets and then use the yarn to loop an announced fractional part. Verify students' responses. Continue with different-sized sets and various fractional parts as time allows.

Fractional parts of a set

Fine-Feathered Fractions

Follow the directions. **Write** the fractions.

1. Color 1 birdhouse blue. 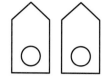 $\boxed{1}$ out of $\boxed{2}$ birdhouses is blue.

2. Color 1 birdhouse red. 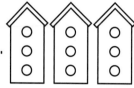 $\boxed{}$ out of $\boxed{3}$ birdhouses is red.

3. Color 1 birdhouse green. 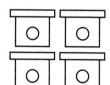 $\boxed{}$ out of $\boxed{}$ birdhouses is green.

Count the birds. **Follow** the directions.

4. Circle the correct fraction.

$\frac{1}{2}$ $\frac{1}{3}$ $\frac{1}{4}$

5. Circle the correct fraction.

$\frac{1}{2}$ $\frac{1}{3}$ $\frac{1}{4}$

6. Color 1 bird. Circle the correct fraction.

$\frac{1}{2}$ $\frac{1}{3}$ $\frac{1}{4}$

7. Color 1 bird. Circle the correct fraction.

$\frac{1}{2}$ $\frac{1}{3}$ $\frac{1}{4}$

Bonus Box: On the back of this sheet, draw 6 birds. Show $\frac{1}{2}$ of them in a tree and $\frac{1}{2}$ of them flying.

©2001 The Education Center, Inc. • *Math Skills Workout* • TEC3225 • Key p. 169

All-Star Fractions

The sky's the limit with this all-star fraction activity!

Purpose: To write fractions for parts of sets

Students will do the following:

- write the total number of items in a set
- count the number of items in a fractional part of a set
- write the fraction for part of a set

Materials for each student:

- copy of page 56
- pencil

Vocabulary to review:

- fraction
- set

Extension activities to use after the reproducible:

- It's easy to monitor students' progress with this fraction writing idea! Give each student an individual chalkboard, chalk, and a cloth or sponge for erasing. To represent ¹/₂, ¹/₃, or ¹/₄, draw an equal number of shapes in a desired number of sets on the classroom chalkboard; circle one set. Ask each youngster to write the corresponding fraction on her chalkboard. At your signal, she displays her answer for your approval. Ask a youngster with the correct answer to write it on the class chalkboard. After students check their responses, erase the board. Repeat the process with sets of various sizes.

- Try this tempting fraction activity! Read aloud *The Doorbell Rang* by Pat Hutchins. Then have volunteers use paper plates and cookie cutouts to dramatize the story as you reread it. To ensure understanding, pause periodically and point out the fractions represented. At the conclusion of the dramatization, have each student imagine that he has treats to share equally with visitors of his own. Assign each student a number of guests and a greater number of treats (be sure that the number of guests divides equally into the number of treats). Give each student a sheet of story paper and have him write and illustrate how he would share the goodies so that each guest has an equal number. Then bind students' resulting pages into a class book that's sure to hit the spot!

Name_____

All-Star Fractions

Meet the all-star fraction players!

Count the stars in each set.
Answer the questions.

1.

a. How many ★ in all? _____
b. How many ★ are in a circle? _____
c. What is the fraction? $\frac{1}{2}$

2.

a. How many ★ in all? _____
b. How many ★ are in a circle? _____
c. What is the fraction? _____

3.

a. How many ★ in all? _____
b. How many ★ are in a circle? _____
c. What is the fraction? _____

4.

a. How many ★ in all? _____
b. How many ★ are in a circle? _____
c. What is the fraction? _____

Bonus Box: On the back of this sheet, draw a set of 4 baseballs. Circle 1 baseball. Write the fraction.

Under the Sea

Reel in linear measurement practice with nonstandard units!

Purpose: To measure length with nonstandard units

Students will do the following:

- estimate length in nonstandard units
- measure length with nonstandard units

Materials for each student:

- copy of page 58
- pencil
- disposable cup holding approximately 10 Goldfish® crackers
- crayon
- small serving of Goldfish crackers for a snack (optional)

Vocabulary to review:

- estimate
- length
- measure

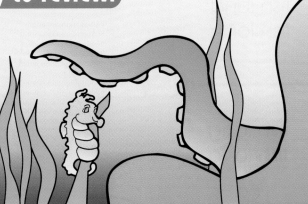

Extension activities to use after the reproducible:

- This center provides a sizable amount of estimation practice! Stock a center with a supply of crayons, cubes, small paper clips, and large paper clips. Prepare a two-column recording sheet that allows space to write an estimated and actual length for each item. Place a class supply of the recording sheet in the center along with a textbook. For each of the four manipulatives, a student estimates how many pieces (end to end) it takes to equal the length of one long side of the book. He records his estimate, uses the manipulatives to check it, and then writes the actual measurement. As the student works, encourage him to use what he learns about measuring with one type of manipulative to make a reasonable estimate for another.

- Here's a tantalizing take-home assignment! Give each student a small resealable plastic bag containing approximately 20 mini marshmallows. Demonstrate how to measure length with the marshmallows by placing them end to end. Instruct each youngster to take her unique measurement tools home and use them to find an item that is longer than ten marshmallows. The next day, invite each student to share her finding with the class. For a sweet conclusion, provide a small serving of marshmallows for each student.

Under the Sea

Estimate how many fish long each line is.
Use the fish to measure.

1.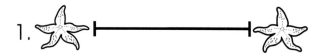

Estimate.   about _____ fish long
Measure.   about _____ fish long

2.

Estimate.   about _____ fish long
Measure.   about _____ fish long

3.

Estimate.   about _____ fish long
Measure.   about _____ fish long

4.

Estimate.   about _____ fish long
Measure.   about _____ fish long

5.

Estimate.   about _____ fish long
Measure.   about _____ fish long

Bonus Box: On the back of this sheet, trace around a crayon. Estimate how many fish long the tracing is. Write. Use the fish to measure. Write.

Note to the teacher: Direct each student to position the provided Goldfish® crackers end to end to measure each line. At the completion of the activity, serve each student a snack of crackers, if desired.

By Leaps and Bounds!

Leap into customary measurement practice with this "toad-ally" awesome activity!

Purpose: To estimate and measure length in inches

Students will do the following:

- estimate the lengths of line segments in inches
- measure line segments with an inch ruler

Materials for each student:

- copy of page 60
- pencil
- inch ruler (or a prepared copy of the inch ruler on page 162)
- crayons

Vocabulary to review:

- inch
- estimate
- measure
- shortest
- longest

Extension activities to use after the reproducible:

- How do your students' estimation skills measure up? Find out with this customary length center! Label a common object such as a pencil with its length. Gather six other objects of various whole-inch lengths. Label a blank card "Answer Key" and list the name and measurement of each unlabeled object. Tuck the key inside an envelope. Place all of the objects, the key, a ruler, and a supply of paper and pencils at a center. To use the center, a student lists the unlabeled objects on a sheet of paper. She estimates each object's length, using the labeled object as a basis for comparison, and records her estimate. Next, she measures each object, records its actual length, and uses the key to check her work.

- Turn customary into extraordinary with this eye-catching display! Cut a supply of wallpaper, construction paper, or wrapping paper into one-inch-wide strips. Give each student a number of assorted strips. Also provide him with a sheet of construction paper, a ruler, scissors, and glue. Instruct each student to cut his strips into one- and two-inch lengths. Ask him to arrange the lengths on the paper in a design of his choice and then glue them in place. Give the youngster a half sheet of writing paper, and ask him to use measurement words to describe the design. Display each youngster's writing and design on a bulletin board titled "Measurement Masterpieces."

By Leaps and Bounds!

Freddy and Fran had a leaping contest. How did they do?
To find out, **estimate** and **measure**.

1 inch

Judge

a.

Estimate. ____ inches   Measure. ____ inches

Freddy

b.

Estimate. ____ inches   Measure. ____ inches

c.

Estimate. ____ inches   Measure. ____ inches

d.

Fran

Estimate. ____ inches   Measure. ____ inches

Look at your work above.
Write each answer.

1. Who made a leap that is 4 inches long? _____

2. How long is Fran's shorter leap? _____

3. How long is the longest leap of all? _____

    Who made it? _____

Bonus Box: On the back of this sheet, draw and color a house that is 3 inches tall. Then draw and color a tree that is 2 inches taller.

 ©2001 The Education Center, Inc. • *Math Skills Workout* • TEC3225 • Key p. 169

Leafy Lengths

Cultivate students' measurement skills with metric practice!

Purpose: To measure length in centimeters

Students will do the following:

- measure with a centimeter ruler
- compare measurements

Materials for each student:

- copy of page 62
- pencil
- centimeter ruler (or a prepared copy of the centimeter ruler on page 162)
- crayons

Vocabulary to review:

- centimeter
- length
- less
- longest

Extension activities to use after the reproducible:

- Students size up the classroom with this partner activity! Prepare a list of 20 or more classroom objects that students can measure with a centimeter ruler. Give each student pair a copy of the list, a sheet of paper, and a centimeter ruler. Have one youngster in each twosome divide the blank paper into two columns labeled "More than 30 centimeters" and "Less than 30 centimeters." Instruct the partners to select eight listed items. Have them measure each item and then write its name and length in the appropriate column. After every twosome has completed its work, invite student pairs to compare their lists.

- Measurement savvy and a bit of luck make this game a winner! To prepare materials for a group of three or four players, place ten pieces of yarn of various whole-centimeter lengths in a small paper bag. Give each player a pencil, a centimeter ruler, and a piece of scrap paper for keeping score. To play one round, each player removes a piece of yarn from the bag, measures it, and announces its length to the group. The player who has the longest piece of yarn earns one point. If two or more players have yarn of equal length, each tied player receives a point. To conclude the round, every player returns his yarn to the bag. Additional rounds are played as time allows. The highest-scoring player wins.

Leafy Lengths

Cathy Caterpillar is hungry! How does her lunch measure up?
Use a centimeter ruler to measure.
Write how many centimeters.

a.

b.

c.

_____ centimeters

_____ centimeters

_____ centimeters

d.

e.

f.

_____ centimeters

_____ centimeters

_____ centimeters

1. **Find** the 2 leaves that are the same length. **Color** them green.
2. **Find** the leaf that is less than 4 centimeters long. **Color** it yellow.
3. **Draw** a star beside the leaf that is 7 centimeters long.

©2001 The Education Center, Inc. • *Math Skills Workout* • TEC3225 • Key p. 169

Bonus Box: How much longer is leaf **e** than leaf **a**? Write your answer on the back of this sheet. Then write a sentence to tell how you decided on your answer.

Bone Mix-Up

This measurement activity is "bone-a-fide" fun!

Purpose: To choose appropriate units of linear measurement

Students will do the following:

- decide whether an item should be measured in inches or feet
- classify items by the appropriate unit of measurement

Materials for each student:

- copy of page 64
- crayons
- scissors
- glue
- quarter sheet of paper

Vocabulary to review:

- inch
- foot
- length
- measure

Extension activities to use after the reproducible:

- How does your classroom measure up? Find out with this small-group activity! Read aloud Leo Lionni's *Inch by Inch,* a charming story about an inchworm that measures nearly everything in his environment. Then have your youngsters measure objects in the classroom environment. To do so, give each group a ruler and a sheet of drawing paper. One student in each group divides the paper into quarters. The group members draw and label a different classroom item in each quarter. For each item, they write the best unit of measurement (inch or foot) below the corresponding drawing. The youngsters test their ideas with the provided ruler, if possible, and make any desired modifications to their work. Bind the groups' completed sheets into a class book titled "How Our Classroom Measures Up."

- Take measurement into the real world without going to great lengths! Provide each student with one green and one blue index card. Instruct her to label the green card "inches" and the blue card "feet." Have each youngster take her cards along with her on a class walk outside. Pause periodically in the walk to point out an item such as a flower or school sign. Ask each student to hold up the card with the unit she thinks would be best for measuring the item. Help students reach consensus. Then continue the measurement walk for a desired period of time.

Bone Mix-Up

Read each bone. **Use** the code to outline it.
Cut along the bold lines. Then **fold** and **glue**.
Put each bone in the correct pocket.

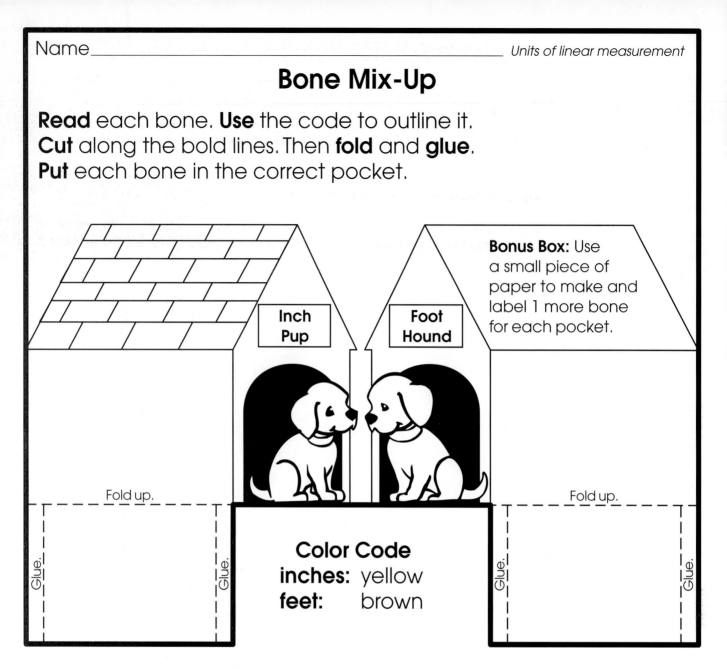

Inch Pup

Foot Hound

Bonus Box: Use a small piece of paper to make and label 1 more bone for each pocket.

Fold up.

Fold up.

Glue.

Glue.

Glue.

Glue.

Color Code
inches: yellow
feet: brown

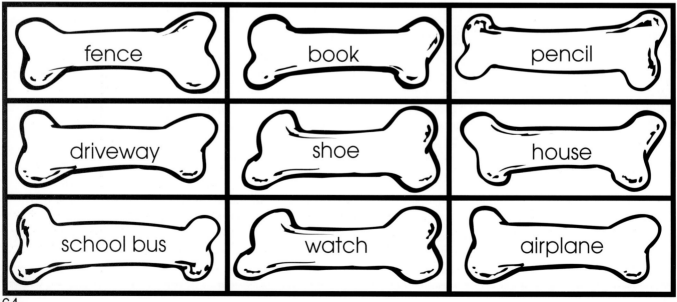

fence	book	pencil
driveway	shoe	house
school bus	watch	airplane

On the Road

This activity gives students truckloads of practice comparing weights!

Purpose: To compare weights using nonstandard units of measurement

Students will do the following:

- compare the weights of objects
- classify objects as weighing more or less than a given object

Materials for each student:

- copy of page 66
- pencil
- crayons
- scissors
- glue

Vocabulary to review:

- weigh
- more than
- less than

Extension activities to use after the reproducible:

- Estimation skills hang in the balance with this small-group activity! Give each group a balance scale, a large wooden block, and three types of manipulatives, such as cubes, tiles, and counters. Also provide a recording sheet that is divided into two columns—one for estimates and one for actual counts. For each type of manipulative, the youngsters estimate how many pieces it will take to equal the weight of the block. They record their estimate, use the balance to check it, and then record the actual number. After every group has completed its work, lead a class discussion about the relative weights of the items.

- This weight center is beyond compare! Form a fist-sized ball of clay, and gather in a basket several objects to compare with the weight of the clay. Label a separate blank card for each of the following headings: "Less Than," "More Than," and "About the Same." Prepare an answer key that states under which category each object fits. Then place the clay, basket, and cards in a center. A student arranges the cards to make three column headings. She holds the clay, picks up one object, and decides how its weight compares to the clay. Then she places the object below the corresponding heading. The youngster sorts the remaining items in a like manner, then uses the provided answer key to check her work.

Name _____

Nonstandard weight measurement

On the Road

Lee's truck only takes things that weigh <u>more</u> than a math book.
Leo's truck only takes things that weigh <u>less</u> than a math book.

Color. Cut along the dotted lines.
Glue each picture on the correct truck.

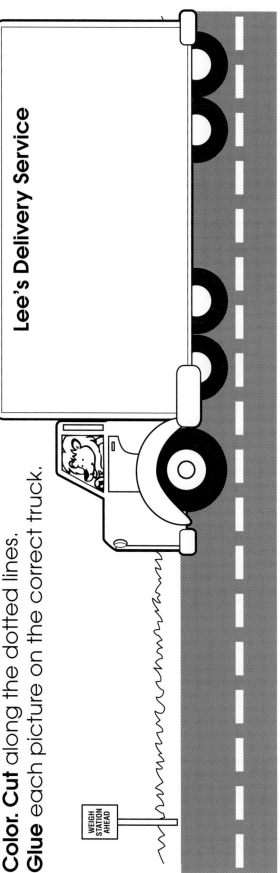

Lee's Delivery Service

WEIGH STATION AHEAD

Leo's Delivery Service

DRIVE SAFELY

Bonus Box: On the back of this sheet, draw and label something in your classroom that weighs more than your shoe. Then draw something in the classroom that weighs less than your shoe.

©2001 The Education Center, Inc. • *Math Skills Workout* • TEC3225 • Key p. 170

Balancing Act

*Use this weight-related activity to tip the scales
in favor of measurement fun!*

Purpose: To compare weights

Students will do the following:

- identify objects as heavier or lighter than a given object
- use a key
- identify the heavier of two objects

Materials for each student:

- copy of page 68
- pencil
- crayons

Vocabulary to review:

- compare
- heavier
- lighter
- pound

Extension activities to use after the reproducible:

- This partner game weighs in as a winner! Give each twosome a balance scale, one die, a supply of wooden cubes, and a sheet of paper for keeping score. To play one round, the first player rolls the die and places the corresponding number of cubes on his designated end of the scale. The second player repeats this process. The player who has the heavier set of cubes earns one point. (If the scale is balanced, each player takes one more turn.) The players clear the scale and continue the game until one player earns five points, becoming the winner.

- Pound for pound, this class activity measures up! Bring an unopened five-pound bag of flour and a bathroom scale to class. Invite each student, in turn, to hold the flour to feel how heavy it is. Divide a sheet of chart paper into two columns. Label one column "More Than 5 Pounds" and the other column "Less Than 5 Pounds." Then display the chart within student reach. Assign students to small groups and give each group two blank cards. Have the group members identify one classroom object for each column, write the name of the object on a card, and then tape the card on the chart. Help volunteers use the bathroom scale to verify the comparative weights for as many of the objects as possible.

Balancing Act

Look at the chart.
Compare each item with a small box of crayons.
Draw an X in the correct box.

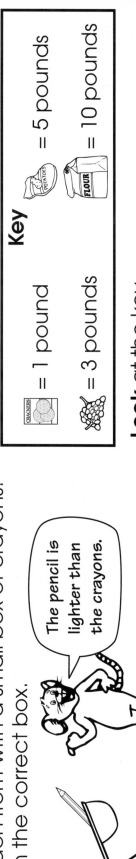

The pencil is lighter than the crayons.

	Heavier Than	Lighter Than
1.		
2.		
3.		
4.		

Key

CRACKERS = 1 pound		POTATOES = 5 pounds	
grapes = 3 pounds		FLOUR = 10 pounds	

Look at the key.
For each pair of items below, **circle** the item that is heavier.

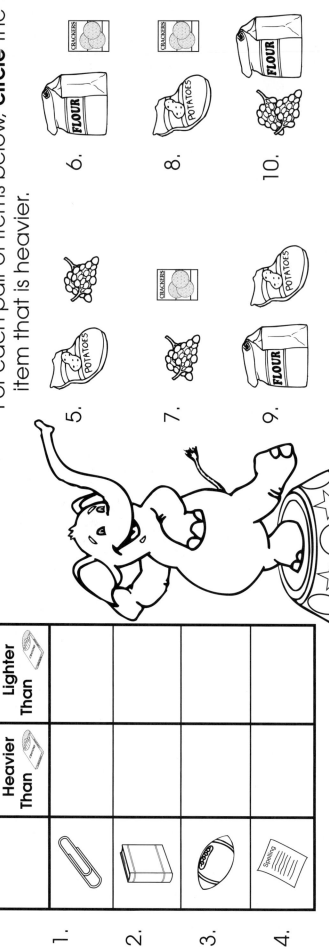

5.   6.

7.   8.

9.   10.

Bonus Box: On the back of this sheet, use the key above to show 1 way to make 15 pounds.

Sweet Treats

Purpose: To explore capacity with nonstandard units

Students will do the following:
- compare the capacities of pictured containers
- indicate the number of containers needed to hold a given quantity

Materials for each student:
- copy of page 69
- pencil
- crayons

Vocabulary to review:
- container
- more
- less

Extension activities to use after the reproducible:

- Provide a week's worth of estimation practice with this quick and easy activity! On Monday, set out a clear plastic container filled with cotton balls. Give each student a blank strip of paper. Have him estimate the number of cotton balls and sign his name. Collect the strips. As you read each strip aloud, record the estimates on the board, grouping any duplicates. After every strip has been read, count the cotton balls aloud and then determine which estimate is the closest. Next, on a displayed sheet of chart paper, have a volunteer write "cotton balls" and the quantity. Repeat this process on each remaining day of the week, filling the container with different items and encouraging students to use the recorded quantities to help them make reasonable estimates.

- Get capacity-measuring skills in order! Letter five containers of different shapes and sizes. Number the bottom of the containers by capacity. Place the containers in random order in a center stocked with paper, a measuring scoop, and a supply of dried beans. A student sequences the containers, beginning with the one she thinks has the least capacity and ending with the one she thinks has the greatest. Next, she determines how many scoops of beans it takes to fill each container. After she records this information on the provided paper, she empties the containers. The youngster makes any desired changes to the sequence of containers. Then she flips the containers to check her work.

Name_____ *Nonstandard capacity measurement*

Sweet Treats

Welcome to Jake's Jelly Bean Store!

Look at each pair of containers.
Color the container that holds more.

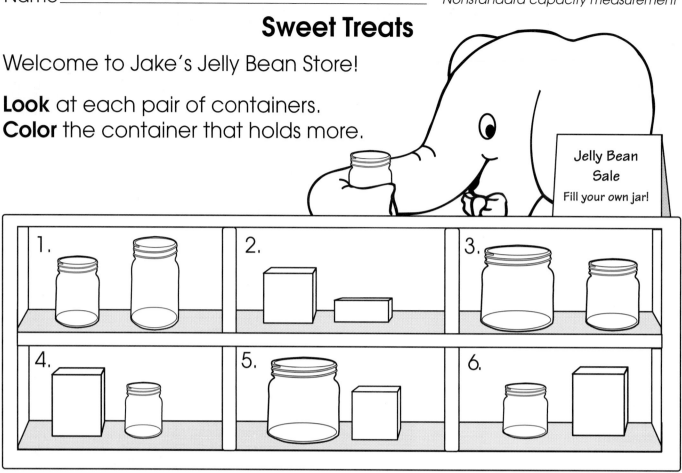

A small jar holds 5 jelly beans.
Color to show how many small jars Jake needs for each customer.

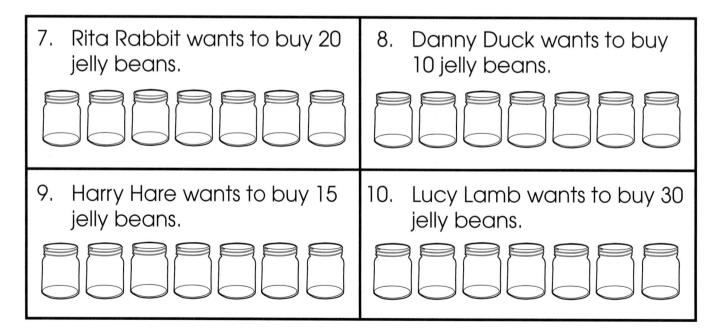

Bonus Box: A small jar holds 5 jelly beans. A large jar holds 10 more jelly beans than a small jar. What is the total number of jelly beans that a large jar holds? Write your answer on the back of this sheet. Then draw a picture of each jar.

Decisions, Decisions!

Purpose: To understand Fahrenheit temperatures

Students will do the following:

- read Fahrenheit temperatures
- classify given temperatures
- identify the most appropriate clothing for given temperatures

Materials for each student:

- copy of page 72
- pencil
- crayons

Vocabulary to review:

- Fahrenheit
- temperature
- degrees

Extension activities to use after the reproducible:

- Appropriate dress is required for this class activity! Program a number of blank cards with temperatures that range from hot to cold. Also gather two pieces (or pictures) of clothing that are appropriate to wear for each of the following weather conditions: warm, hot, cool, and cold. Place them in a box and position the box in an open area. Line up half the class on each side of the box so that the lines face each other. Next, display a card. Have the two line leaders select from the box one piece of clothing that is appropriate for the displayed temperature. After classmates provide feedback about the appropriateness of the selection, have the leaders place the clothing back in the box and return to their places. Continue with the remaining students, reusing the cards as necessary.

- Heat up youngsters' understanding of temperature with picture-perfect posters! Divide students into small groups. For each group, label a 12" x 18" sheet of paper with a different Fahrenheit temperature and an appropriate descriptor such as "warm" or "cold." Provide access to scissors, glue, and a supply of discarded magazines. Instruct the students in each group to cut out pictures of clothing or scenes that correspond with their given temperature. Have them glue the pictures onto the paper to make a collage. After each group has completed its work, enlist students' help to display the collages in order of increasing temperature.

Name _____

Decisions, Decisions!

Read each temperature.
Circle the word that best tells about it.
Look at the box below the bear.
Color the three best pieces of clothing for the bear.

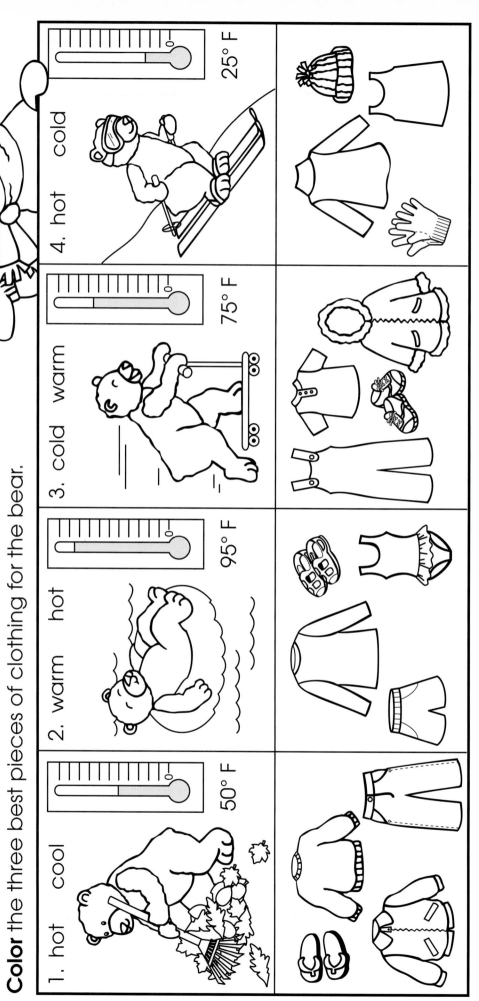

1. hot cool	2. warm hot	3. cold warm	4. hot cold
50° F	95° F	75° F	25° F

Bonus Box: On the back of this sheet, draw a picture of something you like to do outside. Write a sentence about it. Label the picture "hot," "cold," "warm," or "cool" to tell about the weather.

Every Minute Counts!

This classification activity helps students gain a better sense of time lickety-split!

Purpose: To understand the concept of time

Students will do the following:

- classify tasks as taking more or less than one hour

Materials for each student:

- copy of page 74
- pencil
- crayons

Vocabulary to review:

- hour
- minute
- more
- less

Extension activities to use after the reproducible:

- Strengthen students' concept of time with this lively activity! On the board, write a student-generated list of actions that can be done in the classroom, such as clapping hands or hopping on one foot. Give each youngster a piece of scrap paper and then announce a listed action. Have the student estimate how many times she can repeat the action in one minute. After she writes her estimate, time the youngster as she tests it. Instruct her to write the actual number and compare it with her estimate. Repeat the process with a desired number of other listed actions.

- This timely idea is a winner! Divide students into small groups. For each group, label one yellow card "More Than Five Minutes" and another yellow card "Less Than Five Minutes" to make two category titles. Program six white cards with activities that typically require less than five minutes to do, such as closing a door, and six white cards with activities that require more than five minutes to do, such as watching a movie. Instruct each group to place the category cards faceup on a work surface to represent two column headings. Ask the youngsters in each group to read each activity card, discuss how long the activity takes, and then place the card below the appropriate heading. After the sorting is complete, invite each group to tell the class how it classified the activities.

Every Minute Counts!

Read each sentence.
Decide if it takes more or less than 1 hour.
Circle the best answer.

Terry Turtle sees a fly go by.
Harold Hare hops all night.

more	(less)
(more)	less

	more	less
1. Terry Turtle blinks her eyes twice.	more	less
2. Harold Hare and Terry Turtle have a huge pond party.	more	less
3. Harold Hare hops over a log.	more	less
4. Terry Turtle rests on a rock all morning.	more	less
5. Harold Hare writes his name.	more	less
6. Terry Turtle listens to 1 song.	more	less
7. Terry Turtle rides in a boat all afternoon.	more	less
8. Harold Hare races across a room.	more	less
9. Terry Turtle takes a long nap in the sunshine.	more	less
10. Harold Hare eats 1 jelly bean.	more	less

There are 60 minutes in 1 hour.

Bonus Box: Think about the things that Terry Turtle and Harold Hare do. On the back of this sheet, draw a picture of something different that you can do in less than 1 hour. Write a sentence about the picture.

Calendar Caper

Keep students up-to-date with calendar-reading practice!

Purpose: To read and interpret a calendar

Students will do the following:
- distinguish between days and dates
- locate given days and dates on a calendar

Materials for each student:
- copy of page 76
- pencil
- crayons

Vocabulary to review:
- month
- day, date
- first, second, third, last
- before, after

Extension activities to use after the reproducible:
- There's no time like the present for students to explore the concepts of yesterday, today, and tomorrow! Have each student fold a 12" x 18" sheet of construction paper in thirds and then unfold it. Instruct her to label the first section "Yesterday," the second section "Today," and the third section "Tomorrow." Ask her to illustrate and label a corresponding school activity for each section. Allow time for each student to share her work with a classmate. At the end of the following day, have each youngster refer to the activity illustrated in the "Tomorrow" section to check her prediction.

- Before sending monthly school calendars home, use them for this real-life math and writing activity. For each student, staple a copy of a monthly school calendar inside a construction paper folder. On the opposite side, staple a sheet of lined paper. Distribute the folders and invite students to personalize them. Have each youngster study the calendar and write one sentence about each week, including the day and date of any described events. For example, "We are having pizza on Friday, March 15" or "There is a PTA meeting on Thursday, March 21." Encourage each student to share his work with his family members to keep them posted about school happenings.

Calendar Caper

June

Sunday	Monday	Tuesday	Wednesday	Thursday	Friday	Saturday
			1	2	3	4
5	6	7	8	9	10	11
12	13	14	15	16	17	18
19	20	21	22	23	24	25
26	27	28	29	30		

1. What day comes before Saturday? _____
   After Saturday? _____

2. How many Mondays are in June? _____

3. **Find** the first Friday in June. **Color** the box blue.

4. **Find** the third Friday in June. **Color** the box red.

5. **Find** the last Tuesday in June. **Color** the box yellow.

6. What day is June 1? _____

7. **Write** the date of the first Monday in June. _____

_____

Bonus Box: On the back of this sheet, write the months of the year in order. Draw a line under the month it is now. Circle the next month.

©2001 The Education Center, Inc. • *Math Skills Workout* • TEC3225 • Key p. 170

Hickory Dickory Clocks

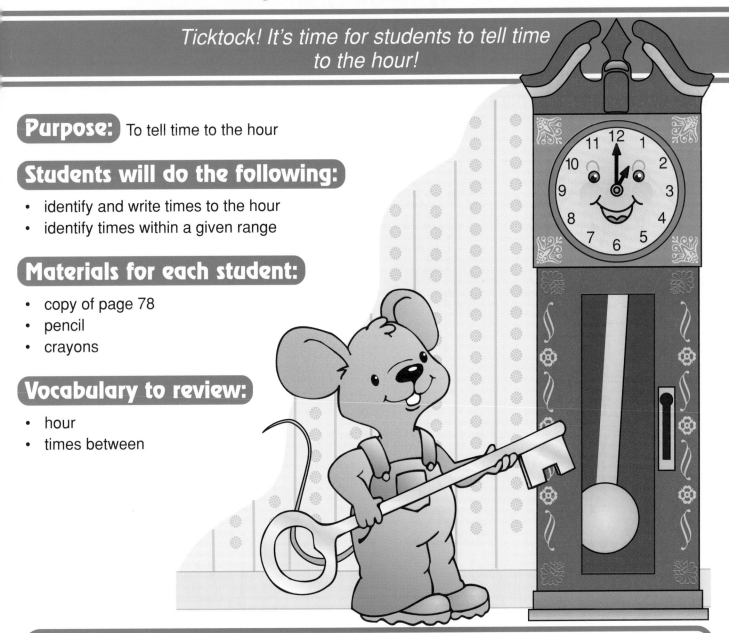

Purpose: To tell time to the hour

Students will do the following:

- identify and write times to the hour
- identify times within a given range

Materials for each student:

- copy of page 78
- pencil
- crayons

Vocabulary to review:

- hour
- times between

Extension activities to use after the reproducible:

- Help students practice telling time to the hour with this nutritious snack! Gather a class supply of dinner-sized paper plates. Make a clockface on each plate by numbering the outer rim 1–12. Cover the plate with plastic wrap. Place a small tortilla and a two- and a four-inch celery stick on the plate. Have each student wash her hands; then give her a prepared plate. Instruct her to position the celery like clock hands to show a given time on the hour. Verify the youngster's response. Repeat the process with a desired number of different times. Then invite each student to spread peanut butter on her tortilla clock. After the youngsters enjoy their tasty snacks, have them remove the plastic wrap; then collect the plates for future time-telling practice.

- Get students' minds ticking with this larger-than-life clock! Number 12 blank cards. To form a clock, seat 12 students in a large circle and distribute the numbered cards sequentially. From the remaining children, select one student to be the time teller and two students to represent clock hands. Have the time teller announce a time to the hour. Instruct the two hands to show the time by lying in the circle (have the minute hand stretch his arms above his head so that he will be longer than the hour hand). Repeat the activity, inviting other students to act as the time teller, hands, and clock numerals.

Hickory Dickory Clocks

Today Mr. Dock will fix clocks that show times
  between 12:00 and 7:00.
Write each time.
Use a crayon to outline each clock that
  Mr. Dock will fix.

1.

2.

3.

4.

5.

6.

7.

8.

9.

Bonus Box: Divide a sheet of paper in half. On one half, draw a picture of something
that you do at 8:00 in the morning. On the other half, draw a picture of something that
you do at 8:00 at night. Label the pictures.

Apple-Picking Time

This bushel of time-telling practice is ripe for the picking!

Purpose: To tell and show time to the hour

Students will do the following:

- read an analog clock and write the time
- draw hands on an analog clock to show a given time
- identify the clock that shows a specified time before or after another time

Materials for each student:

- copy of page 80
- pencil
- red and green crayons

Vocabulary to review:

- o'clock
- after
- before

Extension activities to use after the reproducible:

- What's in the cards? A timely partner activity! Help each youngster make a manipulative clock (see the pattern and assembly directions on page 163). Program each box of a 12-box grid with a different time on the hour. Give each student pair one copy of the grid. One youngster in the twosome cuts the boxes apart, shuffles the resulting cards, and stacks them facedown. Next, a student draws a card and reads the time to himself, without revealing it to his partner. He sets the hands on his clock to represent the time, asks his partner to read it, and then displays the card to verify the answer. The students alternate turns setting and reading the clocks until every card has been used.

- Add a festive flair to a time-telling review! Give each student a copy of a six-inch clock face that does not have hands, a 9" x 12" sheet of construction paper, and a length of curling ribbon. Also provide each youngster with a three-inch square card bearing a time to the hour. The student draws hands on the clock to represent the time and trims the construction paper to make a balloon shape. Then she staples the top of the clock to the balloon, lifts the clock, and glues the card under it. After each youngster tapes a ribbon string to her balloon, display students' work on a bulletin board titled "A Timely Celebration!"

Apple-Picking Time

For each apple, **write** or **draw** the time.

1. ___ : ___

2. ___ : ___

3. _7_ : _00_

4. _5_ : _00_

5. ___ : ___

6. _11_ : _00_

7. ___ : ___

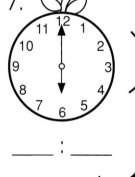

Look at the apples.

Use a red crayon to outline the apple that shows 1 hour <u>after</u> 1:00.

Use a green crayon to outline the apple that shows 2 hours <u>before</u> 6:00.

Bonus Box: Look at number 6. On the back of this sheet, draw a clock that shows the time 3 hours before. Write the time.

©2001 The Education Center, Inc. • *Math Skills Workout* • TEC3225 • Key p. 170

Right on Time!

Purpose: To tell time to the half hour

Students will do the following:

- read an analog clock to the half hour
- write digital time

Materials for each student:

- copy of page 82
- pencil
- crayons

Vocabulary to review:

- hour hand
- minute hand

Extension activities to use after the reproducible:

- Boost students' ability to tell time (and stories!) with this booklet project. Read aloud Eric Carle's *The Grouchy Ladybug*. Prompt discussion about the main character's manners; then invite each student to imagine a friendlier animal character. Give each student two 9" x 12" sheets of white construction paper. Direct her to stack the sheets, hold them vertically, and slide the top paper upward about 1½ inches. Help her fold the papers forward to create graduated layers as shown and then staple along the fold. Guide the student to label each booklet page with a consecutive time to the half hour. Then have her write and illustrate a timely tale about her character, modeling her work after Carle's book.

- Review time to the half hour in a flash! Program a class supply of cards with a variety of times to the half hour. Give one card to each student; then write a time to the hour on the board. If a student has a card bearing the time that is 30 minutes after the displayed time, he stands and holds it up. If he does not, he remains seated. Confirm the responses. Then erase the board and have any standing students sit down. Repeat the process with a desired number of different digital times.

Name _____

Right on Time!

Read each clock.
Write the time.

It is 8:30!

The hour hand is between the 8 and 9.
Trace it with a blue crayon.

The minute hand is on the 6.
Trace it with a red crayon.

1. _ _ : _ _

2. _ _ : _ _

3. _ _ : _ _

4. _ _ : _ _

5. _ _ : _ _

6. _ _ : _ _

7. _ _ : _ _

8. _ _ : _ _

Bonus Box: Look at number 2. On the back of this sheet, draw a clock to show 1 hour later. Use a blue crayon to draw the hour hand. Use a red crayon to draw the minute hand.

Time for Fun!

What's under the Big Top? Bunches of time-telling practice!

Purpose: To tell time to the hour and half hour

Students will do the following:
- draw clock hands to show times to the hour and half hour

Materials for each student:
- copy of page 84
- pencil
- crayons

Vocabulary to review:
- minute hand
- hour hand
- after
- o'clock

Extension activities to use after the reproducible:

- Here's an easy way for students to keep track of time! Tape a lined index card to each student's desk. On the board, list four times during the school day that are on the hour or half hour (be sure to select times at which all of the students are normally in the classroom). Have each youngster copy the times on his card, leaving writing space between them. Ask him to watch the clock throughout the day and note on the card what he is doing at each designated time. At the end of the day, have students compare their notes. If desired, invite students to share their thoughts about how the results might differ on the next school day. Then have them check their predictions.

- There's no time like the present for students to learn how to sequence time! Program a supply of blank cards with digital times to the hour and half hour, labeling each time "A.M." or "P.M." Arrange the cards in chronological order and code the back of each one for self-checking. Shuffle the cards and place them in a center. Arrange for each student to visit the center, sequence the cards, and then flip the cards to check her work. For a more challenging center activity, use an analog clock stamp to program the cards instead of handwritten digital times.

Time for Fun!

Read each time.
Draw clock hands to match.

a. 9:30

b. 7:00

c. 1:30

d. 10:00

e. 3:30

f. 4:30

g. 9:00

h. 12:30

Bonus Box: Use a yellow crayon to color the balloon that says 9 o'clock. Use a blue crayon to color the balloon that shows 30 minutes after 9 o'clock. Use different crayons to color the rest of the picture.

The Big Cheese

Students will scurry to cash in on this coin review!

Purpose: To identify coins and their values

Students will do the following:

- sort pennies, nickels, dimes, and quarters by their values
- identify pennies, nickels, dimes, and quarters

Materials for each student:

- copy of page 86
- pencil
- crayons
- scissors
- glue

Vocabulary to review:

- penny
- nickel
- dime
- quarter
- cents
- coin

The Big Cheese

MENU

Cheeseburger.................50¢
Cheese Pizza ....25¢
Cheese & Crackers...........10¢
Grilled Cheese ....15¢
Cheesecake ....35¢
Cheese Puffs ....1¢

Extension activities to use after the reproducible:

- Presto! This booklet project makes coin identification practice appear right before students' eyes! To make a booklet, a student folds a 6" x 9" piece of construction paper in half. He cuts a sheet of white paper into quarters, stacks the quarters, and staples them inside the construction paper folder. He titles the resulting booklet and then labels one page for each of these coins: pennies, nickels, dimes, and quarters. After every youngster has prepared a booklet, divide students into groups of four. Give each group crayons and at least one coin of each denomination. For each denomination, have each student make a head and a tail crayon rubbing on the corresponding booklet page. Then have students examine the rubbings and share the similarities and differences they notice.

- Sharpen students' observation skills with this hands-on partner center! Place a container of assorted coins and a supply of paper in a center. Have two students sort the coins by denomination. Then instruct the youngsters to compare and contrast the groups of coins, noting their observations on the provided paper. Encourage the youngsters to consider characteristics such as size, color, edges, and imprints. Now that's a coin identification activity you can bank on!

The Big Cheese

Cut along the dotted lines.
Glue each coin on the correct block of cheese.
Use the color code to outline the cheese.

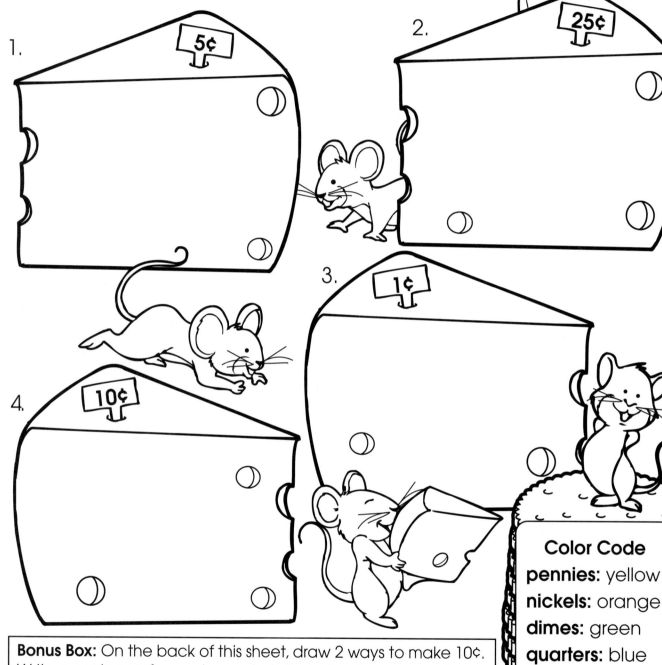

1. 5¢

2. 25¢

3. 1¢

4. 10¢

Color Code
pennies: yellow
nickels: orange
dimes: green
quarters: blue

Bonus Box: On the back of this sheet, draw 2 ways to make 10¢.
Write a sentence for each way to tell what coins you used.

Piggy Bank Math

Cash in on this coin-counting activity for plenty of student learning!

Purpose: To count sets of mixed coins

Students will do the following:

- count mixed sets of pennies, nickels, and dimes
- label a set of coins with the corresponding value

Materials for each student:

- copy of page 88
- pencil
- scissors
- glue

Vocabulary to review:

- penny
- nickel
- dime
- value

Extension activities to use after the reproducible:

- Boost money-counting skills with this "cent-sational" idea! Gather a supply of craft items such as buttons, ribbon, and sequins. Place the items in a designated class store area. Create and post a price list that is appropriate for your students' math skills. Give each youngster a 12" x 18" sheet of white construction paper. Also provide a resealable plastic bag containing a predetermined collection of imitation coins for making purchases. Each student visits the store, selects desired craft items, and counts out the appropriate coins. Then he uses the purchased materials, crayons, markers, glue, and scissors to create an original picture. Math *and* art—what a deal!

- You can bank on this money-trading game to be a winner! Pair students and give each twosome a number die. Give each player a small paper plate for a workmat and a resealable plastic bag containing 20 pennies, five nickels, and five dimes. To play one round, a player rolls the die and places a corresponding number of pennies on her plate. If possible, she trades five pennies for one nickel. Play alternates between players, with each player trading pennies for nickels and nickels for dimes as possible until one player has three dimes. This player earns one point. The game continues with additional rounds until one player earns three points and is declared the winner.

Name _____

Counting sets of coins

7¢	15¢	5¢	12¢	10¢	13¢	20¢

Piggy Bank Math

Mrs. Purdue's class is saving money for a fish tank.
Cut and **glue** to show how much money they have.
(Hint: You will not use 2 of the numbers.)

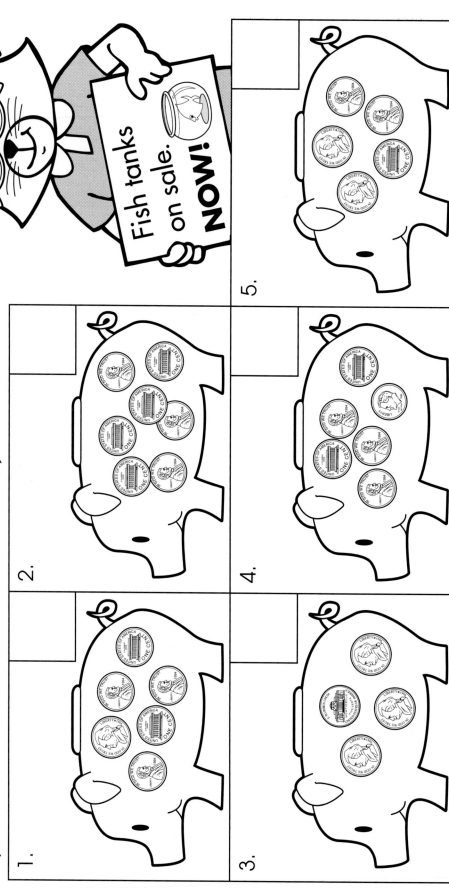

Fish tanks
on sale.
NOW!

1.

2.

3.

4.

5.

Bonus Box: Look at number 3. On the back of this sheet, draw and label a different set of coins that has the same value.

Stock Up!

Purpose: To compare money amounts and prices

Students will do the following:

- count collections of coins
- determine if there is enough money in a collection of coins for a given purchase

Materials for each student:

- copy of page 90
- pencil
- set of real or play coins (if desired, duplicate and cut out the patterns on page 164)

Vocabulary to review:

- penny
- nickel
- dime
- quarter
- cents
- cost
- total

Extension activities to use after the reproducible:

- This bargain of an idea provides coin-counting practice *and* reinforces the concepts of greater than and less than! Use coin stamps to program a piggy bank–shaped cutout with a desired value. Label a class supply of blank cards with prices so that half of the cards have prices that are less than the programmed value and half of them have prices that are greater than the value. Shuffle the cards and stack them facedown. Tape the prepared cutout to the chalkboard; draw and label a chart as shown. Ask each student, in turn, to take a card, read it aloud, and then tape it in the correct column to show how the price compares with the programmed amount.

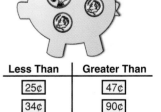

Less Than	Greater Than
25¢	47¢
34¢	90¢
15¢	

- Cash in on your students' money-counting skills to create a "cent-sational" center! Divide students into small groups, and give each group a set of real coins. For each student, provide crayons, a quarter sheet of paper, and a blank card labeled with a different price. Ask the youngster to make a coin rubbing that corresponds with his price. Help him code the back of the rubbing and price card to make the activity self-checking. Collect students' rubbings and cards; then place them in a center. Arrange for two students to visit the center at one time. The youngsters pair each price with the corresponding coin rubbing and then flip the cards and rubbings to check their work.

Comparing money amounts and prices

Stock Up!

Sammy and Sandy have some school shopping to do!
Count each squirrel's money. **Write** each total.
Write "yes" or "no."

School Store

50¢ CRAYONS

25¢ ERASER

40¢ (pen)

85¢ (notebook)

15¢ (pencil)

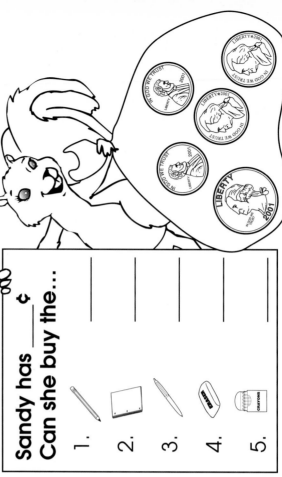

Sammy has _____ ¢
Can he buy the...
1. (pencil) _____
2. (notebook) _____
3. (pen) _____
4. (eraser) _____
5. (crayons) _____

Sandy has _____ ¢
Can she buy the...
1. (pencil) _____
2. (notebook) _____
3. (pen) _____
4. (eraser) _____
5. (crayons) _____

Bonus Box: Does Sammy have enough money to buy a pencil and an eraser at the same time? Use your coins to help you decide. On the back of this sheet, write a sentence to tell your answer.

©2001 The Education Center, Inc. • *Math Skills Workout* • TEC3225 • Key p. 171

Fast-Food Freddy

Try this activity made-to-order for matching coin and money amounts!

Purpose: To identify the coins needed for a given purchase

Students will do the following:

- read prices less than $1.00
- count sets of coins
- color the coins needed for purchases

Materials for each student:

- copy of page 92
- pencil
- crayons

Vocabulary to review:

- penny
- nickel
- dime
- price
- set

Extension activities to use after the reproducible:

- Count on this center to be a great investment in your students' money skills! Use adhesive labels to cover the prices on a selected page of an advertising circular for toys. Program each label with a price that corresponds with your students' money-counting abilities. Next, letter three library-card pockets. Draw details on them so that they resemble clothing pockets. Inside each pocket, place a different combination of play coins that is equal to or greater than two of the prices. (If desired, use prepared construction paper copies of the coin patterns on page 164.) Write the total on the back of the pocket for self-checking. Place the prepared ad and pockets at a center stocked with paper and pencils. For each pocket, a student writes the corresponding letter on a sheet of paper, counts the coins, and then writes the total. She flips the pocket to check her work. She determines for which items she has enough money and then writes the name of the item she would most like to buy.

- Strengthen youngsters' problem-solving skills with this coin-combination activity! On an overhead transparency, write a coin-related question, such as "If a piece of candy costs 10¢, what two coins can be used to buy it?" Instruct each student to write and illustrate his answer on provided paper. After every student has responded, invite a volunteer to write his answer on the transparency and explain how he determined it. If desired, have him use a set of overhead coins to illustrate his answer.

Fast-Food Freddy

Freddy's restaurant has the best
   prices in town!
Read the prices.
Color the coins needed
   to buy each food.

Remember,
1 dime
equals 10¢.

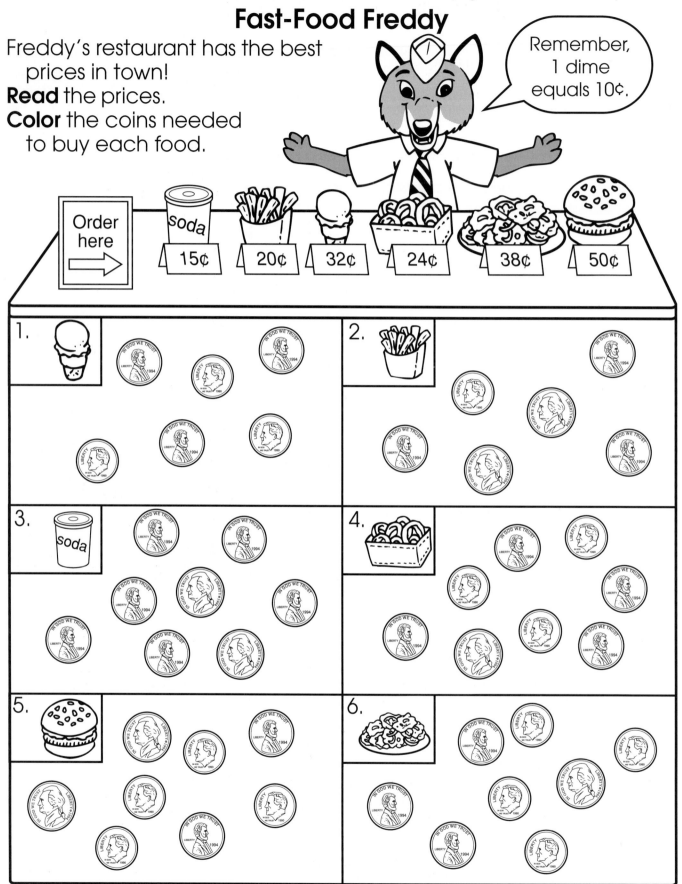

Order here ⟶

soda 15¢
20¢
32¢
24¢
38¢
50¢

1.

2.

3.

4.

5.

6.

Bonus Box: Look at the prices above. How much would it cost to buy french fries and a soda? On the back of this sheet, write and illustrate your answer.

Pocket Puzzler

This handy reproducible provides pockets full of money-counting practice!

Purpose: To use the fewest coins possible to show given amounts

Students will do the following:

- group coins to show given amounts
- show given amounts with the fewest coins
- classify groups of coins by the number of coins

Materials for each student:

- copy of page 94
- pencil
- scissors
- glue
- crayons

Vocabulary to review:

- fewest
- amount
- coins
- cents

Extension activities to use after the reproducible:

- Introduce the concept of equivalent sets of coins with this class activity! Vertically list the following coins on the chalkboard: pennies, nickels, dimes, and quarters. Help students determine how many of each coin are needed to make 50¢ if only that type of coin is used. Record the numbers. Point out that as the value of the coin increases, the number of coins decreases. Then prompt discussion about reasons it is helpful to know equivalent sets of coins, such as the convenience of carrying two quarters rather than 50 pennies!

- An element of chance puts a spin on this partner game! Program each of 15 blank cards with a different coin amount between 10¢ and 99¢. Prepare a paper clip spinner like the one shown. Provide each player with a set of play coins (if desired, use the patterns on page 164). To play, the players stack the cards facedown. The first player draws a card and reads it aloud. Each player represents the amount with her coins and then reveals how many coins she used. If the players used the same number of coins, the card is placed in a discard pile. If not, the first player spins the spinner. The player who represented the amount with either fewer or more coins, as indicated by the spinner, earns the card. Play alternates until one player earns five cards and is declared the winner.

Pocket Puzzler

Cut along the dotted lines.
Use the fewest coins to show each amount.
Glue the coins.
Color the pockets by the code.

Color Code
1 coin: green
2 coins: orange
3 coins: red
4 coins: yellow

Nails
3¢ per lb.

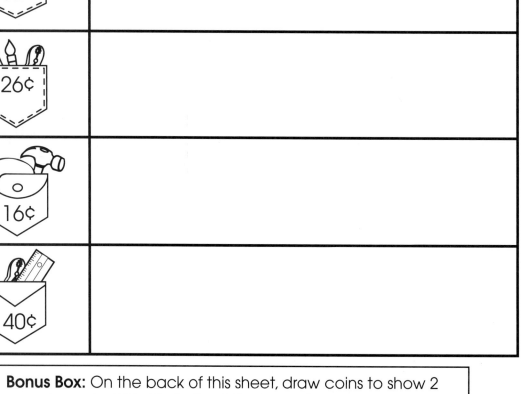

1. 20¢

2. 32¢

3. 26¢

4. 16¢

5. 40¢

Bonus Box: On the back of this sheet, draw coins to show 2 ways to make 25¢. Circle the 1 that uses fewer coins.

Money Math

This money-related activity is a sound investment in addition and subtraction skills!

Purpose: To add and subtract money amounts

Students will do the following:

- draw coins to show addition and subtraction of money amounts
- complete addition and subtraction sentences that use money amounts

Materials for each student:

- copy of page 96
- pencil

Vocabulary to review:

- add
- subtract
- cents
- plus
- minus
- equals

Extension activities to use after the reproducible:

- Here's a literature-based idea that puts subtraction practice into a real-life context! Read aloud *Alexander, Who Used to Be Rich Last Sunday* by Judith Viorst. Then examine how Alexander spends his money by setting a dollar's worth of overhead coins on an overhead projector. Reread the book, pausing after each time Alexander spends money to have a volunteer adjust the coins accordingly. With students' input, write the corresponding subtraction sentence on the chalkboard. At the book's conclusion, point out that even though Alexander's expenses are small, together they make a big difference!

- Dish up mouthwatering addition practice! In advance, make an ice-cream flavor price list similar to the one shown. Prepare a number of ice-cream scoop cutouts in the corresponding colors. Give each student an ice-cream cone cutout, a predetermined set of play coins, and a blank sheet of paper. Have her count the coins and then refer to the menu to write an order that she can afford with the money. After the student totals the cost of the order, verify her work and help her make the purchase. Next, ask the youngster to use the purchased materials and the provided cone cutout to assemble and glue an ice-cream treat on a sheet of drawing paper. After she labels the treat with the total cost, celebrate your students' wise (and flavorful!) shopping by serving a yummy ice-cream snack.

Ice-Cream Flavors		
chocolate 5¢	vanilla 3¢	strawberry 6¢

Money Math

Complete each chart.

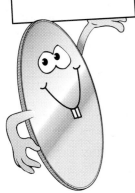

	Look.	Add.	Draw.	Write.
1.	10¢	2¢	⑩ ① ①	10¢ + 2¢ = ____¢
2.	7¢	1¢		7¢ + 1¢ = ____¢
3.	15¢	3¢		15¢ + 3¢ = ____¢
4.	12¢	1¢		12¢ + 1¢ = ____¢
5.	25¢	2¢		25¢ + 2¢ = ____¢

	Look.	Subtract.	Draw.	Write.
6.	12¢	2¢	⑩ ⊗ ⊗	12¢ – 2¢ = ____¢
7.	15¢	10¢		15¢ – 10¢ = ____¢
8.	7¢	2¢		7¢ – 2¢ = ____¢
9.	20¢	10¢		20¢ – 10¢ = ____¢
10.	16¢	5¢		16¢ – 5¢ = ____¢

Bonus Box: Jane finds 3 pennies. Her aunt gives her a quarter. How much money does she have now? On the back of this sheet, write and illustrate an addition sentence to show your answer.

Spot the Shapes!

Set your students on a shape-filled trail with this fetching activity!

Purpose: To identify plane figures

Students will do the following:

- color plane figures by a code
- distinguish between plane figures that have more than three sides and those that do not

Materials for each student:

- copy of page 98
- pencil
- crayons

Vocabulary to review:

- circle
- triangle
- square
- rectangle
- hexagon
- side
- corner

Extension activities to use after the reproducible:

- Stretch students' shape identification skills! Give each student a Geoboard and a large rubber band. Have her use the rubber band to make a shape with three sides on the Geoboard. Then invite several volunteers to show the class their shapes. Lead students in a discussion about the number of sides and corners the shapes have as well as their various sizes and shapes. Point out that the size and shape of the displayed figures vary, but they are all triangles. Repeat the process, asking students to create figures with four and then five sides. Review or introduce the names of the resulting figures as appropriate. Now that's a nifty way to help students identify the distinguishing features of common shapes!

- This eye-catching display shows that shapes are everywhere! Read aloud *The Shape of Things* by Dayle Ann Dodds. Revisit the book with students, asking volunteers to point out the shapes featured in the collage illustrations. Next, provide access to templates of common shapes, construction paper, crayons, glue, and scissors. Have each student use the provided materials to make an illustration of a scene that incorporates two or more of the shapes. Invite him to show the class his completed illustration and challenge his peers to identify the shapes included. Then display students' creative work below the title "Can You Spot the Shapes?"

Spot the Shapes!

Spot needs help to find his way to the bones!
Color by the code.
Begin at the ★.
Connect all the shapes that have more than 3 sides.

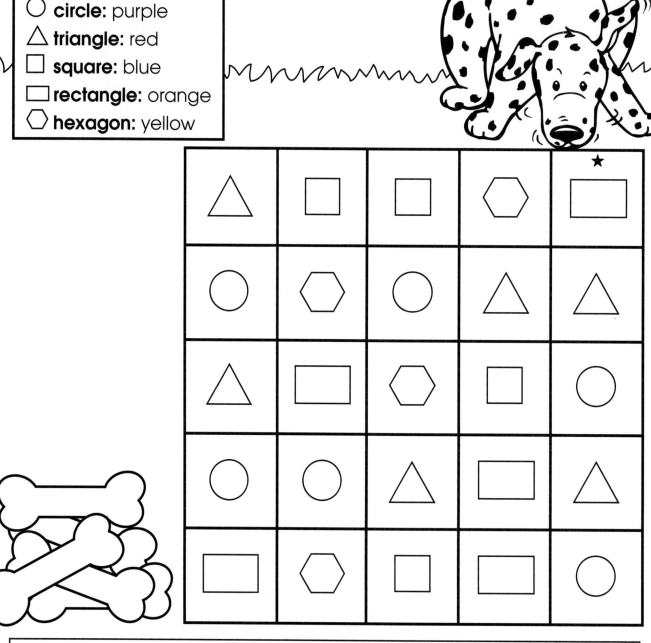

Color Code
○ **circle:** purple
△ **triangle:** red
☐ **square:** blue
▭ **rectangle:** orange
⬡ **hexagon:** yellow

Bonus Box: On the back of this sheet, draw a triangle. Write a sentence that tells how many sides and corners it has.

Just the Solid Facts!

Purpose: To recognize solid figures

Students will do the following:

- identify solid figures with the same shapes as pictured real-life objects
- color by a code
- identify which objects have six faces

Materials for each student:

- copy of page 100
- pencil
- crayons

Vocabulary to review:

- cube
- sphere
- pyramid
- cone
- cylinder
- rectangular prism
- face

Extension activities to use after the reproducible:

- This classification activity helps students feel right at home with solid figures! Give each student two unlined index cards. Instruct him to find two solid objects at home and then draw each one on a separate card. Have each youngster return the completed cards by a designated date. Choose one or more attributes by which to classify the objects, such as the number of faces or whether the objects roll or stack. Use yarn lengths to divide a bulletin board into the number of columns appropriate for the chosen classification system. Label the columns. Then help students tack their cards in the correct columns.

- Round up some practice in identifying distinguishing attributes! Use two yarn lengths to create a large Venn diagram on the floor. Program each of two blank cards with a selected attribute of solid figures, such as straight sides, curved sides, or ability to roll. Place one card inside each circle. Have each student select a small solid object from the classroom (or cut a picture of a solid object from a discarded magazine). Seat students around the Venn diagram. Ask each student, in turn, to determine whether her object (or picture) belongs outside the Venn diagram or in a section of it. Have her position it in the corresponding place. Invite volunteers to verbally summarize the information portrayed by the completed diagram. Now that's a larger-than-life way to get students' classification skills in shape!

Just the Solid Facts!

Color the objects to match the code.
Find each object that has 6 faces.
Draw an X on the matching handle.

Bonus Box: On the back of this sheet, draw a different object that is the shape of a cube. Write a sentence that tells how many faces it has.

©2001 The Education Center, Inc. • *Math Skills Workout* • TEC3225 • Key p. 171

Shell Shapes

Provide practice matching plane and solid figures with this "turtle-rific" reproducible!

Purpose: To match plane figures with faces of solid figures

Students will do the following:

- identify and color a flat face of a given solid figure
- color to match plane figures with faces of solid figures

Materials for each student:

- copy of page 102
- pencil
- crayons

Vocabulary to review:

- square
- circle
- triangle
- rectangle
- face

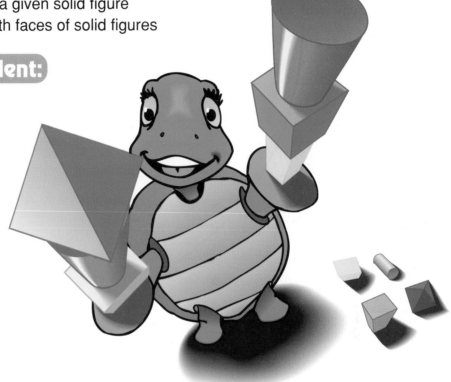

Extension activities to use after the reproducible:

- What's in the bag? A hands-on geometry activity! Place a circle, a square, and a triangle attribute block in a paper lunch bag. Gather a number of solid objects that each have at least one flat face. Seat students in a circle. To begin, hold up an object and direct students' attention to one of its faces. Then give the bag to a student. Ask her to reach inside the bag without looking and remove the block that has the same shape as the face. After verifying the response, have the youngster return the block to the bag and pass the bag to the youngster on her right. Continue until every student has taken a turn (reuse the objects, as necessary). What a kid-pleasing way to help students get a feel for plane and solid figures!

- The relationship between plane and solid figures becomes clear with this activity! Divide students into small groups. Give each group several solid objects, each of which has at least one flat face. For each student, provide crayons and a sheet of drawing paper. The student traces a flat face of each object and labels each tracing with the name of the object. Then the group members verbally compare the number of sides and corners of their tracings. To conclude the activity, invite each group to show the class its objects, point out a face on each one, and tell the number of sides and corners the face has.

Name _____

Identifying plane figures as faces of solid figures

Shell Shapes

Read each color word below.
Color the shaded face on each object.
Look at Tess Turtle's shell.
Color each shape the correct color.

Look for these sights!

blue

purple

red

orange

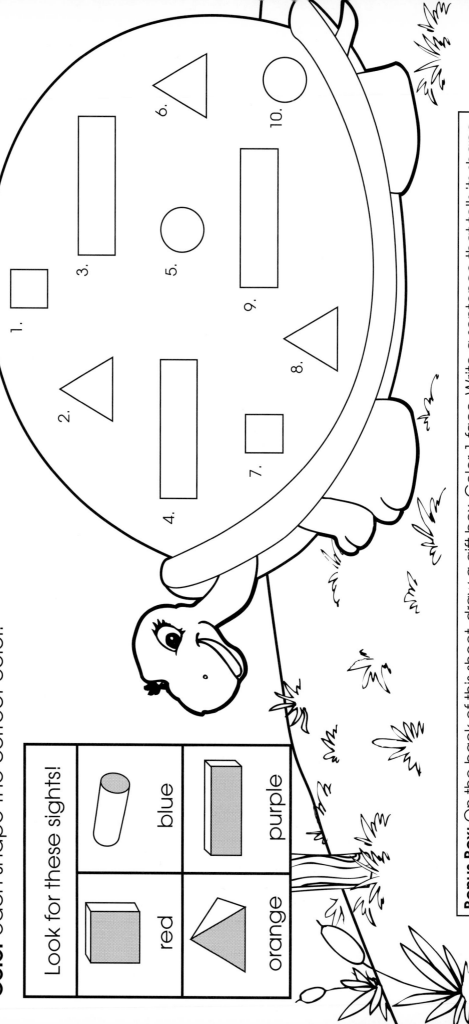

1.

2.

3.

4.

5.

6.

7.

8.

9.

10.

Bonus Box: On the back of this sheet, draw a gift box. Color 1 face. Write a sentence that tells its shape.

©2001 The Education Center, Inc. • *Math Skills Workout* • TEC3225 • Key p. 171

A Shower of Shapes

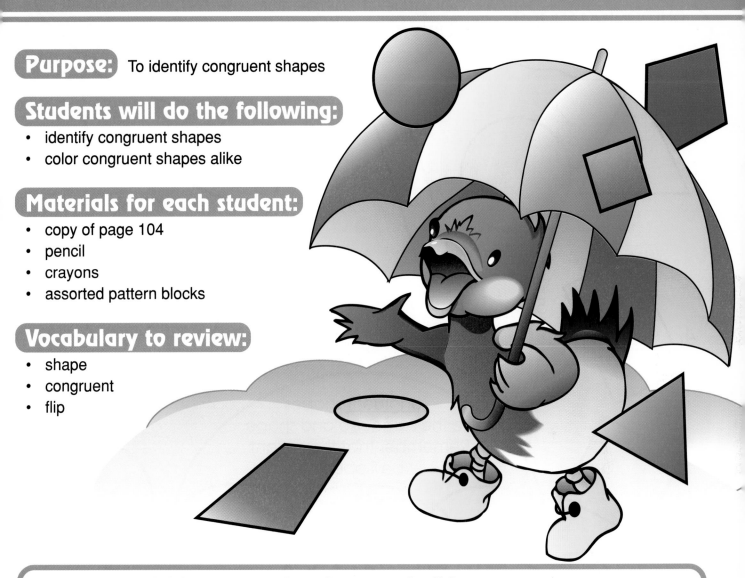

Purpose: To identify congruent shapes

Students will do the following:

- identify congruent shapes
- color congruent shapes alike

Materials for each student:

- copy of page 104
- pencil
- crayons
- assorted pattern blocks

Vocabulary to review:

- shape
- congruent
- flip

Extension activities to use after the reproducible:

- Put a creative twist on congruency! Provide access to templates of several different shapes. Give each student a sheet of paper. Instruct her to trace a chosen template twice so that the tracings do not overlap. Then have her use crayons to incorporate the tracings into a picture. Bind students' completed work into a class book titled "Find the Congruent Shapes!" Challenge students to point out the congruent shapes hidden in each unique picture.

- Energize math time! To prepare, make a class supply of shape cutouts so that each cutout is congruent to exactly one other cutout. Gather your students outside in a large circle and randomly distribute the shapes. Ask one student to stand in the center of the circle and announce an attribute of his shape. If a student does not have a shape with the announced attribute, he sits down. If he does, he remains standing. The student in the center approaches a standing student. The class chants "Join with me and we will see if our shapes have congruency" as the youngster places his shape atop the shape the chosen classmate holds. If the shapes are congruent, the two youngsters run around the outside of the circle once. If they are not congruent, the student in the center repeats the process. After the congruent shape has been identified, select the next student to stand in the center and continue play.

A Shower of Shapes

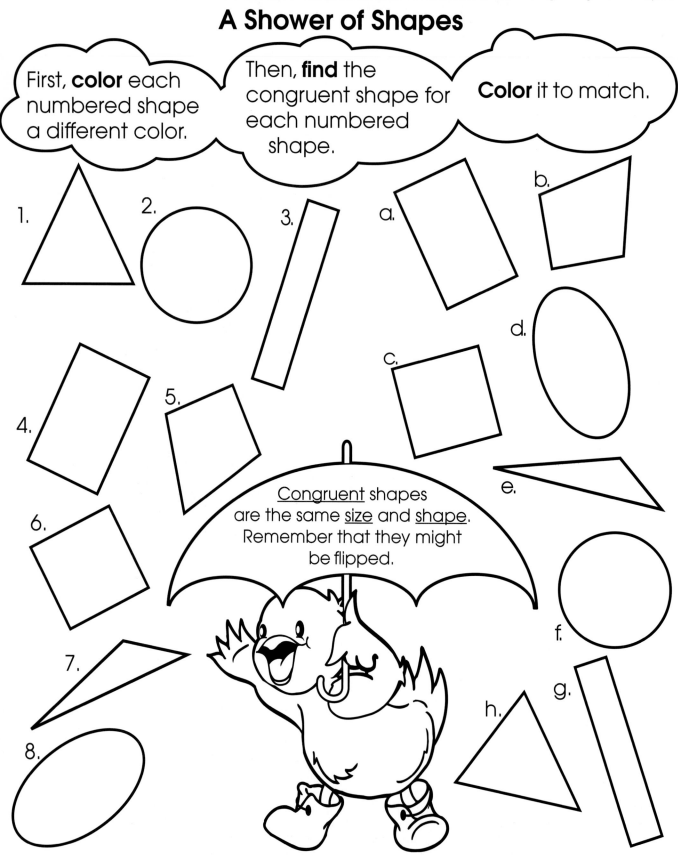

First, **color** each numbered shape a different color.

Then, **find** the congruent shape for each numbered shape.

Color it to match.

1.

2.

3.

a.

b.

c.

d.

e.

4.

5.

6.

7.

8.

Congruent shapes are the same <u>size</u> and <u>shape</u>. Remember that they might be flipped.

f.

g.

h.

Bonus Box: On the back of this sheet, use pattern blocks to trace your own shower of congruent shapes. Have a friend color each pair of congruent shapes a different color.

Snazzy Symmetry

Show students how to keep in step with symmetry!

Purpose: To recognize lines of symmetry

Students will do the following:

- identify lines of symmetry
- draw lines of symmetry
- complete symmetrical figures

Materials for each student:

- copy of page 106
- pencil
- crayons

Vocabulary to review:

- symmetry
- matching sides
- figure

Extension activities to use after the reproducible:

- Here's a nifty way to get students in line with symmetry! Give each student a Geoboard, crayons, two rubber bands of different colors, and a dot paper grid (if desired, duplicate page 165 and cut the patterns apart). Provide time for each youngster to experiment with creating symmetrical figures, using one rubber band to outline a figure on the Geoboard and one rubber band to show its line of symmetry. Next, have the student display his favorite figure on the Geoboard. Ask him to use crayons to copy it on the dot paper. Compare the dot paper and Geoboard figures for accuracy, and guide the youngster to make any needed corrections. Then encourage him to take the dotty example of symmetry home to share with his family.

- Showcase students' symmetry skills with this creative project! Prepare a class supply of symmetrical butterfly-shaped cutouts. Provide each student with glue, a cutout, and a supply of sequins and small pom-poms. To create a symmetrical design, have the youngster position several sequins and pom-poms on one butterfly wing as desired. Then instruct her to repeat the design on the other wing. After she confirms that her design is symmetrical, have her glue the materials in place. Allow time for the eye-catching projects to dry; then display them on a bulletin board titled "Flying High With Symmetry!"

Snazzy Symmetry

Look at the butterfly.
Circle each shape that shows 2 matching sides.

Look at each picture.
Draw a line to show matching sides.

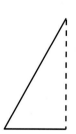  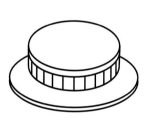 

For each figure, **draw** the matching side.

  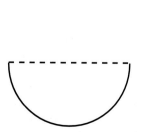 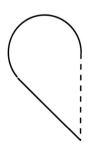

Bonus Box: On the back of this sheet, write 2 capital *H*s. On each *H*, use a crayon to show a different way to make matching sides.

Patterns Ahoy!

Delight your young mateys with this pirate-themed reproducible laden with patterns!

Purpose: To copy and continue geometric patterns

Students will do the following:

- copy a geometric pattern
- continue geometric patterns
- color geometric patterns

Materials for each student:

- copy of page 108
- pencil
- crayons

Vocabulary to review:

- pattern
- copy

Extension activities to use after the reproducible:

- Share the eye-opening book *Lots and Lots of Zebra Stripes: Patterns in Nature* by Stephen R. Swinburne to introduce your students to patterns found in nature. To follow up the photo-illustrated book, provide each student with a sheet of drawing paper, a pencil, and a mobile writing surface such as a clipboard. Then take the class on a walk outside to find natural patterns. When a student finds a pattern, have him draw a picture of it. Upon return to the classroom, ask each student to color his favorite pattern and then describe it on a separate sheet of paper. Encourage him to also identify the pattern with a label such as ABCABC, if appropriate. Your students are bound to see the world as they've never seen it before!

- Double the patterning fun at a partner center titled Double Me! To prepare, place two sentence strips and a container of pattern blocks in a center. Have one student arrange several blocks on a sentence strip to create a pattern. Then direct his partner to use additional blocks to duplicate the pattern on a different sentence strip. After the students verify that the pattern has been copied accurately, ask them to clear the sentence strips, switch roles, and repeat the activity. For a fun variation, provide paper clips, pom-poms, buttons, and other unique manipulatives for students to transform into interesting patterns.

Name _____

For number 1, **copy** the pattern.

For numbers 2–5, **continue** the patterns.

Then **color** each pattern you see on the ship.

Patterns Ahoy!

1. △ ○ △ △ ○ △

2. ▭▯ ▯ ○ ▢ ▭▯ ▯ ○

3. △ ▢ △ △ ▢ △

4. △ ○ △ △ ○ △

5. ▭ ◇ ▭ ▭ ◇ ▭

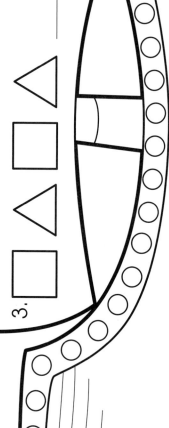

Bonus Box: Captain Pete the Parrot needs a belt! On the back of this sheet, draw a belt for him. Decorate it with a pattern of coins and jewels.

Next in Line

Use this shapely reproducible to help students' patterning skills fall in line!

Purpose: To continue and describe patterns

Students will do the following:

- continue geometric patterns
- describe geometric patterns

Materials for each student:

- copy of page 110
- pencil
- sheet of paper

Vocabulary to review:

- pattern
- triangle
- circle
- rectangle
- shape

Extension activities to use after the reproducible:

- Teamwork comes into play with this patterning idea! Divide students into groups of three. Give each student several crayons, a sentence strip, and a blank card that has been programmed with a pattern such as ABAB or AABB. Ask each youngster to sign her strip and then turn it over. Beginning at the left edge of the strip, the student draws several shapes to illustrate her assigned pattern. Then she trades strips with a group member. The student draws several more shapes to continue the pattern her classmate drew. She trades her classmate's strip with the third group member, continues the pattern on the strip she receives, and then returns the strip to its original owner. After each student checks her continued pattern, display all of the strips to share the colorful results of teamwork!

- Reel in pattern-describing skills with this "fin-tastic" activity! Read aloud *Pattern Fish* by Trudy Harris, encouraging students to chime in with the predictable text. Then provide access to fish-shaped templates, construction paper, scissors, and glue. Direct each youngster to use the materials to make a fish that is decorated with a geometric pattern. Display students' completed fish on a bulletin board titled "Fishy Patterns" and number the fish for easy reference. Then invite each student to verbally describe his pattern and challenge his classmates to identify the number of the corresponding fish. What a surefire way to hook students on patterns!

Next in Line

Draw the next shape for each pattern.

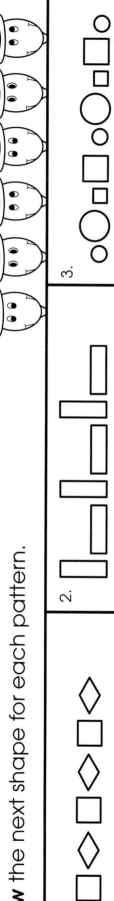

1.
2.
3.

4.
5.
6.

7.
8.
9.

Look at the pattern on the picnic basket.
Complete the sentence to tell about the pattern.

10. The pattern on the basket is _____

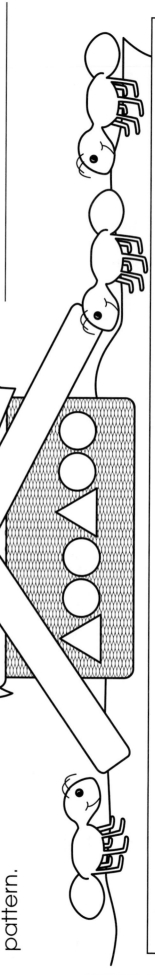

©2001 The Education Center, Inc. • _Math Skills Workout_ • TEC3225 • Key p. 172

Bonus Box: Look at pattern number 7. Copy the pattern on another sheet of paper. Write a sentence that tells about it.

Patterns on the Mend

*Have students correct these shapely quilts to "sew"
up an understanding of patterns!*

Purpose: To analyze and correct geometric patterns

Students will do the following:

- identify incorrect shapes in patterns
- draw the correct shapes to complete patterns
- color patterns

Materials for each student:

- copy of page 112
- pencil
- crayons

Vocabulary to review:

- pattern

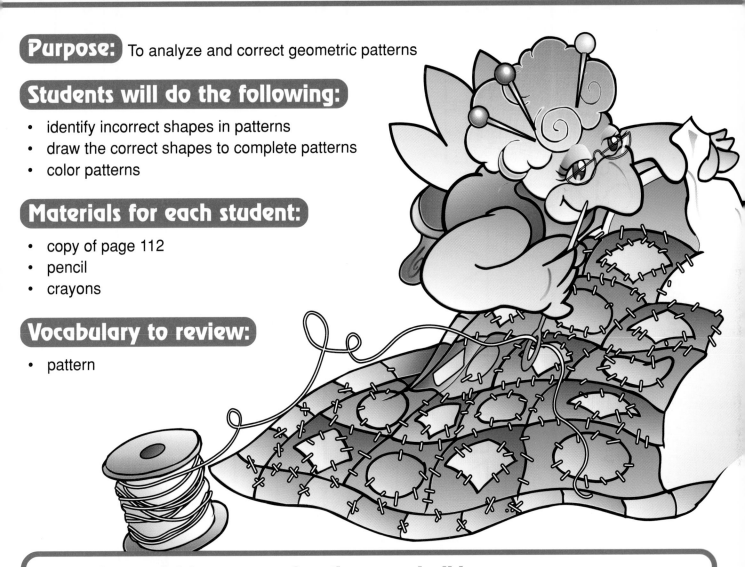

Extension activities to use after the reproducible:

- Build students' patterning skills with this partner activity! Give each pair of students a 9" x 12" sheet of tagboard and a supply of assorted Unifix® cubes. The first youngster folds the tagboard in half and then opens it slightly to stand it between the second student and himself. He connects several cubes to make a pattern, using the tagboard to keep the pattern from his partner's view. Then the youngster removes one cube and replaces it with a different-colored cube to create a mistake in the pattern. Next, he reveals the pattern to the second student and challenges her to identify and correct the mistake. After she corrects and verbally describes the pattern, the students trade roles. The activity continues for a desired number of turns.

- If you have calendar time in your class, this pattern idea is for you! Program two sets of seasonal cutouts with the dates 1–31. Use selected cutouts to display the dates on the calender so that the cutouts make a pattern, such as *apple, apple, leaf.* Place the remaining cutouts nearby in a container. Each day before students arrive at school, remove one cutout from the calendar and replace it with the cutout in the container that has the same date. At an appropriate time during your calendar routine, challenge students to identify and correct the pattern error. You can be sure that students will enjoy looking for your "mistake"!

Name _____

Patterns on the Mend

For each quilt, **draw** an X on the incorrect shape.
Draw the correct shape below it.
Color the quilts to show patterns.

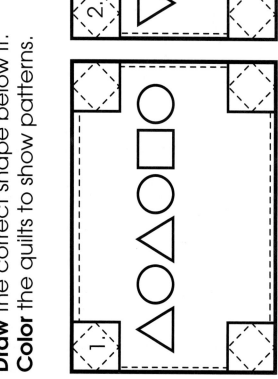

1. △ ○ △ ○ □ ○

2. □ △ ▽ △ □ ▽ △

3. □ □ □ □ □ □ □ □

4. □ □ △ △ ○ □ △ △

5. □ □ ○ ○ □ ○ □ ○

6. □ ○ ○ □ ▭ ○ □ ○ ○

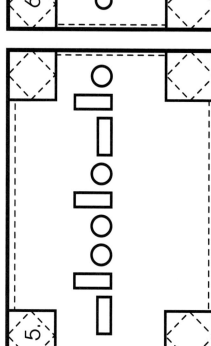
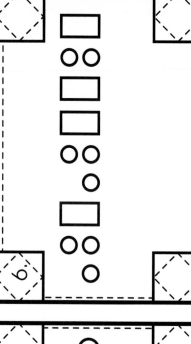
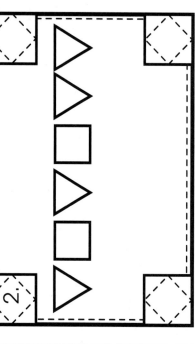

Bonus Box: On the back of this sheet, draw and color a quilt with a different pattern. Write a sentence to tell about the pattern.

Slam Dunk Patterns

This number-pattern lineup is bound to score big with students!

Purpose: To complete number patterns

Students will do the following:

- count by twos and fives
- complete number patterns
- classify number patterns

Materials for each student:

- copy of page 114
- pencil
- scissors
- glue
- red crayon
- blue crayon

Vocabulary to review:

- pattern
- skip-counting

Extension activities to use after the reproducible:

- Counting by twos makes it easy to keep score! Divide the class into two equal-size teams. For each team, label a scorekeeping area on the chalkboard, and position an empty wastebasket at the front of the classroom. Instruct each team to line up single file in front of its basket. Then give each line leader a sponge ball. To play, each line leader stands a designated distance from her team's basket and tries to toss the ball into it. If she is successful, she earns two points. If she is not successful, she earns no points. The player returns to her seat, and the game continues with the remaining players. Each player who makes a basket updates her team's score by writing the appropriate multiple of two below the previous score. At the game's conclusion, lead your students in reading the number patterns displayed. Declare the team with the higher score the winner.

- High fives for number patterns! Have each student trace his hand on a 9" x 12" sheet of construction paper. Instruct him to cut out the tracing. Next, help the class tape their cutouts in a row on the chalkboard. Invite students to predict how many high fives there are. Then sequentially label each cutout with a multiple of five as the class counts along. Compare the final number with the predictions. What a handy way to boost skip-counting skills!

Slam Dunk Patterns

Cut along the dotted lines.
Glue to complete each pattern.
Use the color code to draw an X beside each row.

Cut-out pieces (top row): 10 · 22 · 15 · 6 · 14 · 25 · 15 · 12 · 30 · 16

Color Code
twos: red
fives: blue

a. 2 · 4 · □ · 8 · □ · 12

b. 10 · □ · 14 · □ · 18 · 20

c. 5 · 10 · □ · 20 · □ · 30

d. □ · 20 · 25 · □ · 35 · 40

e. 12 · □ · 16 · 18 · 20 · □

Bonus Box: On the back of this sheet, draw a pair of sneakers for each student in the class. Count by twos to label them. Write a sentence that tells how many sneakers there are in all.

Spidery Patterns

Spin some kid-pleasing pattern practice with this "spider-ific" activity!

Purpose: To complete and continue number patterns

Students will do the following:

- count by fives and tens to complete and continue number patterns
- classify number patterns

Materials for each student:

- copy of page 116
- pencil
- yellow crayon
- orange crayon

Vocabulary to review:

- pattern
- fives
- tens
- least
- greatest

15 20 25 30 35 40

Extension activities to use after the reproducible:

- Keep students on the move with this skip-counting activity! Program each of several 9" x 12" sheets of tagboard with a consecutive multiple of ten. Sequentially place the resulting number cards facedown in a row on the floor. Have a volunteer stand behind each card. Instruct the child behind the first card in the row to pick it up and show it to the class. Then announce the name of another child in line. Challenge the seated students to determine the child's number by counting up by tens. Have the child hold up her card to check their prediction(s) and then return it to its original position. Repeat the process with the remaining students in line. Select a new group of students for another round of skip-counting fun!

- Students will flip over this form of skip-counting assessment! Fold a 12" x 18" sheet of construction paper in half lengthwise. Make cuts in the top layer to make ten flaps as shown. Beginning with "5," write a sequential multiple of 5 under each flap. Lay the folded paper on a work surface. Place a cube on a flap other than the first one. Ask the student to lift the first flap, read the number, and then count by fives to determine the number under the marked flap. Have him lift the marked flap to check his answer. Close the flaps, place the cube on a different flap, and then repeat the process. Now that's a revealing number-pattern idea!

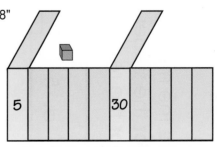

Spidery Patterns

Write the missing numbers.
Color the spider's legs by the code.
Color the rest of the spider any way you wish.

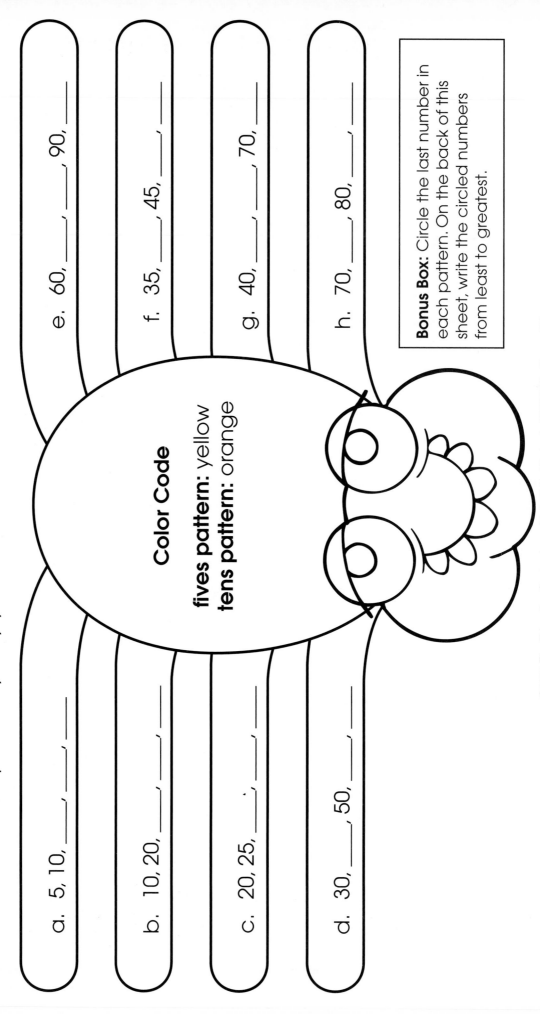

a. 5, 10, ____, ____, ____

b. 10, 20, ____, ____, ____

c. 20, 25, ____, ____, ____

d. 30, ____, 50, ____, ____

e. 60, ____, ____, 90, ____

f. 35, ____, 45, ____, ____

g. 40, ____, ____, 70, ____

h. 70, ____, 80, ____, ____

Color Code

fives pattern: yellow
tens pattern: orange

Bonus Box: Circle the last number in each pattern. On the back of this sheet, write the circled numbers from least to greatest.

Pattern Wisdom

This "tree-mendous" pattern activity is something to hoot about!

Purpose: To complete and continue number patterns

Students will do the following:

- count by twos, fives, and tens to complete and continue number patterns

Materials for each student:

- copy of page 118
- pencil
- orange crayon

Vocabulary to review:

- number pattern
- odd

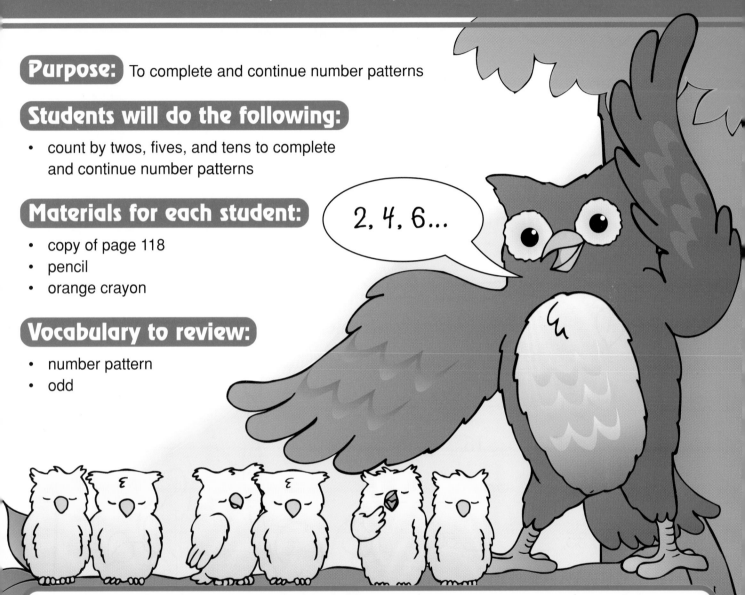

2, 4, 6...

Extension activities to use after the reproducible:

- Round up skip-counting practice with this small-group activity! Have each group of students sit in a circle. Give one student in each group an individual chalkboard, a piece of chalk, and an eraser. To play one round, announce "two," "five," or "ten" to indicate the type of number pattern. Ask the student with the board to write the number and then pass the materials to the student on her left. Have this student write the next number in the pattern and then pass the materials. Continue in this manner for a desired period of time. Ask each group to read its pattern aloud; then have the next youngster in each circle erase the board and begin a new pattern.

- This pattern activity provides all sorts of skill-boosting fun! To prepare, divide a bulletin board into three columns. Label one column for each of the following: twos, fives, and tens. Program a class supply of blank cards so that each card has a different task. Use the following format: "Start with [number]. Count by [twos, fives, or tens]." Give each student a card and half a sentence strip. Instruct her to write five numbers on the strip according to the card's directions. Ask the student to show the class her strip and challenge her classmates to identify the pattern. Then have her post the strip on the bulletin board in the appropriate column.

Pattern Wisdom

Complete each number pattern.

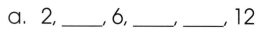

Whooo! Whooo! **Count** by tens, fives, or twos!

a.   2, ____, 6, ____, ____, 12

b.   5, ____, ____, ____, 25, ____

c.   ____, 20, ____, 40, ____, ____, 70

d.   ____, 10, 15, ____, ____, 30, ____

e.   8, 10, ____, 14, ____, 18, ____

f.   30, 40, ____, ____, 70, ____, ____

g.   25, ____, 35, ____, ____, 50

Bonus Box: Look at the numbers above. Circle each odd number with an orange crayon. On the back of this sheet, write a sentence that tells what you notice about patterns **b, d,** and **g.**

Busy Bees

What's all the buzz? Why, it's a sweet approach to missing addends!

Purpose: To identify missing addends

Students will do the following:

- count on 1, 2, or 3 to determine missing addends
- complete addition number sentences

Materials for each student:

- copy of page 120
- pencil
- crayons

Vocabulary to review:

- addition sentence
- count on

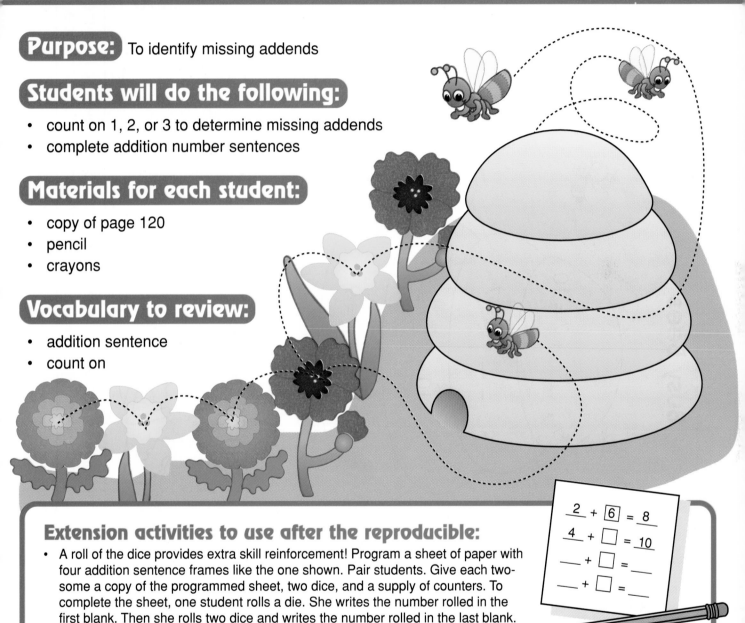

Extension activities to use after the reproducible:

- A roll of the dice provides extra skill reinforcement! Program a sheet of paper with four addition sentence frames like the one shown. Pair students. Give each twosome a copy of the programmed sheet, two dice, and a supply of counters. To complete the sheet, one student rolls a die. She writes the number rolled in the first blank. Then she rolls two dice and writes the number rolled in the last blank. Her partner uses the manipulatives to determine the missing addend and writes it in the box. The students alternate turns rolling the dice to complete the sheet.

- Draw on students' creativity for this missing addend project! For each student, fold a 12" x 18" sheet of white paper in half lengthwise. In the top layer, make two cuts to the fold to make three equal-sized flaps. Label the first flap with either "1," "2," or "3" to represent an addend and the third flap with a number from 4 to 12 to represent a sum. To complete his project, a student labels the middle flap with a question mark. He draws the corresponding numbers of objects under the first and third flaps. The youngster determines the missing addend and draws the appropriate number of objects under the middle flap. On the back of the middle flap, he writes the addition sentence illustrated. Display students' completed projects with the flaps closed. Challenge classmates to determine the missing addends. Then have them lift the corresponding flaps to check their answers.

Busy Bees

Read the addition sentences.
Use the flowers to count on 1, 2, or 3.
Write the missing numbers.

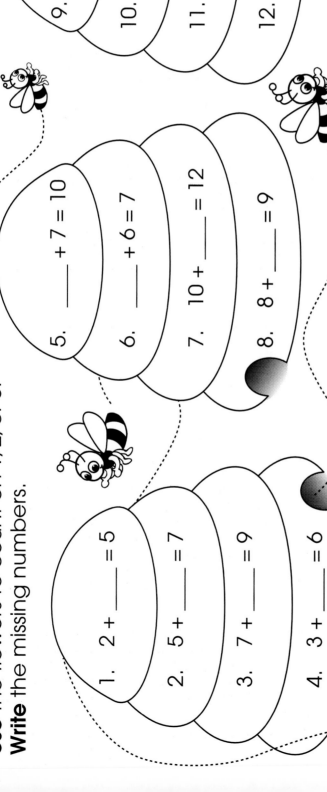

1. 2 + ___ = 5
2. 5 + ___ = 7
3. 7 + ___ = 9
4. 3 + ___ = 6

5. ___ + 7 = 10
6. ___ + 6 = 7
7. 10 + ___ = 12
8. 8 + ___ = 9

9. ___ + 9 = 11
10. 5 + ___ = 8
11. ___ + 8 = 10
12. 9 + ___ = 12

1 2 3 4 5 6 7 8 9 10 11 12

Bonus Box: There are 2 bees on the flowers. More bees come. Now there are 6 bees in all. On the back of this sheet, draw a picture of the bees and flowers. Write a matching addition sentence.

Delicious Data

Use this tempting activity to give your students the sweet taste of graphing success!

Purpose: To interpret a picture graph

Students will do the following:

- read a picture graph
- interpret a picture graph

Materials for each student:

- copy of page 122
- pencil
- crayons

Vocabulary to review:

- more
- most
- fewest
- equal

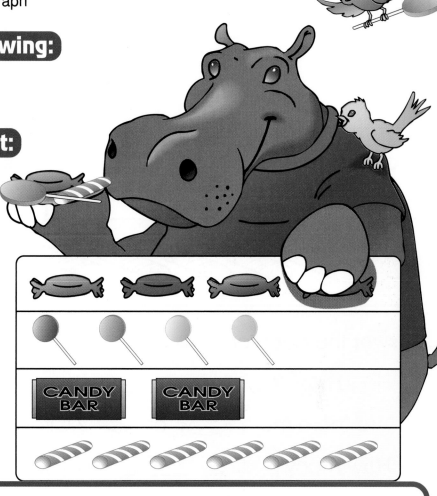

Extension activities to use after the reproducible:

- This versatile idea keeps graphing interest high all year! Post a laminated speech bubble cutout on a bulletin board titled "Question of the Week." Add a head-and-torso cutout that you have personalized to resemble yourself. Use a wipe-off marker to program the speech bubble with a question about a preference, such as "Do you like green or red apples more?" Have each student respond by illustrating his answer on a provided paper square. Help the youngsters tack their illustrations on the board to create a picture graph. Throughout the week, guide the class in verbally analyzing the graph. For more graphing practice, replace your likeness with a student's self-portrait. Help the featured student reprogram the speech bubble. Repeat the activity each week until every student has had a turn to ask a question.

- Sorting and graphing go hand in hand with this partner activity! Give each twosome a supply of assorted buttons, a sheet of writing paper, and a sheet of construction paper. Instruct each student pair to sort its buttons by a chosen characteristic, such as color or number of holes. Have the youngsters arrange the buttons on the construction paper to form a picture graph. Then ask them to write two or more sentences that tell about the graph. If desired, have each student pair position its written work beside the graph; then ask every youngster to quietly walk along an established classroom route to visit each graph display.

Delicious Data

Look at the graph.

Answer the questions.

1. How many? a. 🍬 _____   b. 🍬 _____

2. Are there more 🍬 or 🍬 ? Circle the answer.   🍬   🍬

3. How many? a. 🍭 _____   b. CANDY BAR _____

4. How many more 🍭 than CANDY BAR ? _____

Follow the directions to color the graph.

5. Use a red crayon. Color the candy that has the most pieces.

6. Use an orange crayon. Color the 2 kinds of candy that have an equal number of pieces.

7. Use a yellow crayon. Color the candy that has the fewest pieces.

Bonus Box: Look at the graph. How many more candy bars are needed to equal the number of lollipops? Write a sentence on the back of this sheet to tell your answer.

©2001 The Education Center, Inc. • *Math Skills Workout* • TEC3225 • Key p. 173

A Splash of Color

Purpose: To record and interpret data on a picture graph

Students will do the following:

- record data on a picture graph
- interpret a picture graph

Materials for each student:

- copy of page 124
- crayons
- scissors
- glue
- pencil

Vocabulary to review:

- data
- graph
- most
- least

Extension activities to use after the reproducible:

- How do you make the most of transition time? Line up some math reinforcement! When it's time for students to line up in preparation for leaving the classroom, announce two categories, such as students wearing sneakers and those who are not. Have your youngsters form lines to correspond with the categories. Point out that the lines represent data, much as a picture graph does. Lead the class in analyzing the data before leaving the room. Now that's a handy way to make math real!

- This timesaver makes graphing a class act! On a vinyl tablecloth, use a permanent marker to draw horizontal lines approximately eight inches apart to make a blank grid for a picture graph. Then to establish a supply of graphing ideas, give each student a lined index card. Have her write on the card a possible topic for a class graph, such as favorite fruits or how students get to school. Collect the cards and store them in an empty recipe box. To make a graph, read a selected card aloud, framing the topic in the form of a question. Ask each student to draw his response on a blank index card. Spread the prepared tablecloth on the floor, label each row as appropriate, and have each youngster place his drawing in the correct row. After a class discussion about the data collected, clear and fold the grid for future use. Easy to store, easy to use!

Recording and interpreting data on a picture graph 123

Recording and interpreting data on a picture graph

A Splash of Color

Mr. Bright has used a lot of paint!
Color the paint cans.
Cut them out.
Glue the paint cans on the graph.

The Number of Cans Used			
red			
blue			
green			

Answer the questions.

1. What color did Mr. Bright use the most? _____

2. What color did Mr. Bright use the least? _____

3. How many more cans of blue than green did Mr. Bright use? _____

4. How many cans of red and blue did Mr. Bright use in all? _____

Bonus Box: Look at the graph above. How many cans of blue and green paint did Mr. Bright use in all? On the back of this sheet, write a number sentence to show your answer. Draw a picture to go with your work.

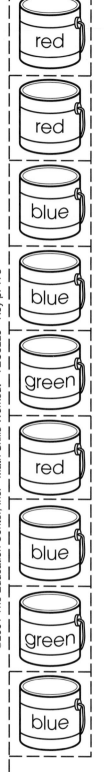

red

red

blue

blue

green

red

blue

green

blue

Tilly's Tally

Purpose: To complete and interpret tally tables

Students will do the following:

- use tally marks to record data
- interpret a tally table

Materials for each student:

- copy of page 126
- pencil
- crayons

Vocabulary to review:

- tally mark
- table
- total

Extension activities to use after the reproducible:

- Spark class discussions with this daily tally activity! Display a laminated sheet of poster board within student reach. Use a wipe-off marker to write a yes-or-no, opinion-based question near the top of the poster board. Below the question, draw two columns. Label one column "Yes" and the other column "No." To answer the question, have each student make a tally mark in the appropriate column. Ask a volunteer to total the tally marks for each column and announce the results. Then invite youngsters to tell how they answered the question and why. Not only will students gain valuable math practice, but they'll also gain a greater awareness of their classmates' viewpoints!

- The element of chance makes this small-group game a winner! To prepare the materials for one group, place three different-colored sets of ten counters in a lunch bag. Give each youngster a sheet of paper. Have her divide it into three sections and label one section for each color. In turn, each student shakes the bag and then removes a counter without looking inside. She makes a tally mark in the appropriate section and returns the counter to the bag. Play continues in a like manner until one player accumulates ten tally marks for any one color and is declared the winner.

Name_____

Tilly's Tally

Count Tilly's eggs and chicks.
Use tally marks to complete the table.
(Hint: Remember that $|$ *= 1 and* $\cancel{||||}$ *= 5.)*

Look at the table. **Answer** the questions.

1. How many chicks does Tilly have? _____

2. How many eggs are in Tilly's nest? _____

3. How many chicks and eggs are there in all? Use tally marks to show your answer. _____

4. Imagine that 1 more chick hatches. How would Tilly use tally marks to show the total number of chicks? _____

Bonus Box: On the back of this sheet, draw and color more farm animals. Then make a tally table to show how many there are of each kind.

©2001 The Education Center, Inc. • *Math Skills Workout* • TEC3225 • Key p. 173

Go-Kart Graphing

Purpose: To record and interpret information on a bar graph

Students will do the following:

- use tally marks to record data on a bar graph
- complete a bar graph
- interpret a bar graph

Materials for each student:

- copy of page 128
- pencil
- crayons

Vocabulary to review:

- tally marks
- total
- bar graph
- most
- fewest

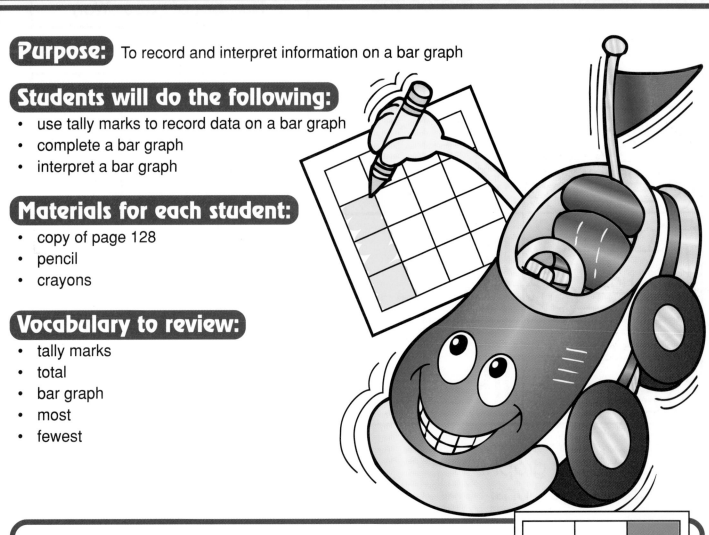

Extension activities to use after the reproducible:

- What makes a good bar graph? Your students are sure to have the answer after this class activity! Display an unlabeled and untitled bar graph similar to the one shown. Ask students to tell what the graph shows. Students will undoubtedly discover that they do not have enough information to interpret the graph. As youngsters identify the graph's missing elements (title, column labels, and row labels), add the elements to the graph to reflect data about a desired topic. When the graph is complete, verbally analyze it as a class. Then guide the students in creating a class reference that summarizes the key elements of a bar graph.

- When it comes to quick and easy graphing activities, count on common manipulatives to provide plenty of possibilities! Remind students that a bar graph can be horizontal or vertical and that it should have labels and a title. Pair students. Give each twosome a sheet of paper and a desired number of assorted pattern blocks or other manipulatives of various colors. Have the youngsters sort the manipulatives by color. Next, instruct the twosome to create a bar graph that shows the number of manipulatives in each color group. Then ask the students to write two sentences about their graph on the back of their paper.

Go-Kart Graphing

Look at the tally marks.
Write the totals.
Color the bar graph to match the totals.

Number of Races Won		Total
Speedy	𝍸𝍷 𝍷	
Flash	|||	
Lightning	𝍸𝍷	

Number of Races Won

	Speedy	Flash	Lightning
6			
5			
4			
3			
2			
1			
0			

Look at the bar graph.
Answer the questions.

1. Which car won the most races? _____

2. Which car won the fewest races? _____

3. How many races did Lightning win? _____

   How many more races did Speedy win? _____

4. How many races were there in all? _____

Bonus Box: On the back of this sheet, write a number sentence that tells how many races Speedy and Lightning won in all.

A Matter of Chance

This hands-on approach to probability is likely to be a winner with your students!

Purpose: To understand and apply basic concepts of probability

Students will do the following:

- make predictions
- conduct a probability experiment

Materials for each student:

- copy of page 130
- copy of the cards on page 166
- paper lunch bag
- pencil
- crayons
- scissors

Vocabulary to review:

- probability
- predict
- more often

Extension activities to use after the reproducible:

- The concept of probability gives this idea a happy ending! In advance, place eight red cubes and two blue cubes in an opaque container and select two storytime books. Tell the class that the container has ten cubes—some red and some blue. If a red cube is chosen, you will read the first book. If a blue cube is chosen, you will read the second book. Ask students to predict which color will be chosen; then draw a cube. Return the cube to the container and then share the appropriate story. On each of several days, repeat the process with the same container and different books. Then invite students to share their ideas about the number of red and blue cubes. After revealing the container's contents, guide students to conclude that red cubes were more likely to be drawn because there were more of them.

- Put a spin on probability! Prepare a copy of the spinner wheel on page 166. Demonstrate how to use a paper clip and pencil to spin it. Pair students. Give each twosome a copy of the spinner wheel. The youngsters color each section a different color and then cut out the spinner wheel. Next, they predict which colors the spinner will land on more and less often. The first student spins the spinner, and the second student records the color on which the spinner lands. The students switch roles and repeat the activity for nine more spins. Then they compare their predictions with the results.

A Matter of Chance

Help Tommy Tiger and Chelsey Cheetah learn about probability!

Part 1

Cut the cards apart.

How many are there? _____

How many are there? _____

Place the cards in the bag.

Predict which kind of card you will get more often.

Circle your prediction.

How to play:

1. **Take** a card from the bag.

2. **Color** a ☐ to tell which kind of card you got.

3. **Put** the card back in the bag.

4. **Repeat** Steps 1–3 until each ☐ is colored.

Part 2

How many did you get? _____

How many did you get? _____

Circle the kind of card that you got more often.

Why do you think you got this card more often? _____

_____

Bonus Box: Imagine that Tommy and Chelsea play the same game with 8 new cards. They get more striped than spotted cards. Draw the new cards on the back of this sheet. Write a sentence that tells why you drew them this way.

Prized Pets

Purpose: To use logical reasoning to solve problems

Students will do the following:

- use logical reasoning
- match pets with the best descriptions

Materials for each student:

- copy of page 132
- pencil
- crayons

Vocabulary to review:

- clue
- first
- second
- third

Extension activities to use after the reproducible:

- Enhance logical reasoning with this classy thinking game! For one round, invite three students to stand at the front of the classroom. Explain to the seated students that you will provide clues about one of the youngsters who is standing, and they need to determine who the clues best describe. Announce the clues, taking care to proceed from general to more specific ones. Then challenge the seated students to identify the described youngster. Invite volunteers to explain their reasoning. After the class correctly identifies the described youngster, ask the students at the front of the room to return to their seats. Play additional rounds as time allows.

- Your young sleuths will be eager to solve this mystery! Conceal a common item in a bag. On the chalkboard draw a T chart with "yes" and "no" columns. Tell students that their job is to use as few clues as possible to determine what is in the bag. Next, describe the hidden item with a statement such as "It is round" or "It is not heavy." Record the clue on the chart. Continue in a like manner with two more clues. Then invite a student to read the list aloud. Challenge the class to guess the mystery item. If the class does not correctly identify it after three guesses, provide additional clues as needed. After the correct answer is provided, remove the mystery item from the bag. Case solved!

Name_____

Prized Pets

Read each clue below.
Write each prize number on the correct line.

A.

First goes to a pet with 2 ears.

Second goes to a pet with a long, scaly tail.

Third goes to a pet that hops.

B.

First goes to a pet that sings.

Second goes to a pet with 4 legs.

Third goes to a pet that purrs.

C.

First goes to a pet that likes water.

Second goes to a furry pet.

Third goes to a pet with a hard shell.

Bonus Box: Choose 1 pet from each group above. On the back of this sheet, draw the 3 pets. Write a different clue for each one. Then write 1 clue that is true for all 3 pets.

Mind Stretchers

Take students' logical reasoning skills to new heights with this brain-boosting activity!

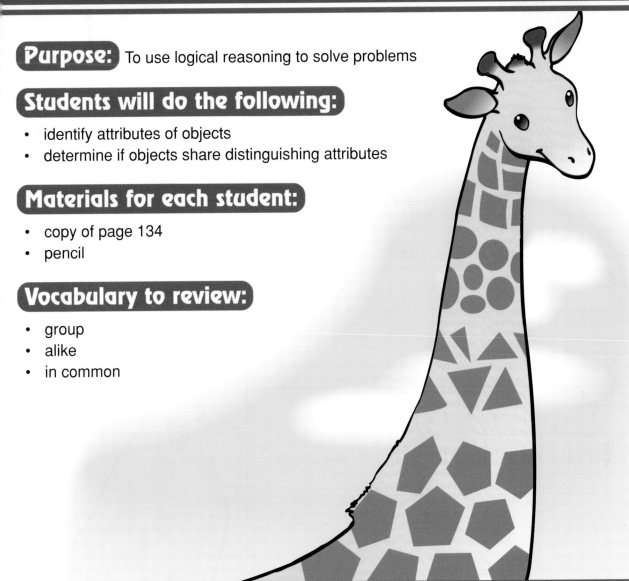

Purpose: To use logical reasoning to solve problems

Students will do the following:

- identify attributes of objects
- determine if objects share distinguishing attributes

Materials for each student:

- copy of page 134
- pencil

Vocabulary to review:

- group
- alike
- in common

Extension activities to use after the reproducible:

- Promote flexible thinking with this sorting idea! Pair students. Give each twosome a collection of small assorted objects, such as buttons, shells, or novelty erasers. The first student secretly chooses an attribute and sorts the objects accordingly. Next, he challenges the second student to identify his sorting method. After she correctly identifies it, the second student sorts the objects by a different attribute and asks the first youngster to identify the new sorting method. Now that's a creative way to put logical reasoning to the test!

- This warm-up activity helps students get their classification skills in tip-top shape! Prior to a math lesson, write several numbers (or words) on the chalkboard, secretly grouping them by chosen attributes. Possible attributes include single and double digits, even and odd, or straight and curved lines. Allow time for students to silently analyze the similarities and differences among the numbers (words). Then invite volunteers to share their ideas and reasoning. Confirm all logical responses, pointing out that there might be more than one correct answer. No doubt students' interest will be sparked by the brainteaser, so be sure to repeat the activity on other days.

Name _____

Mind Stretchers

Complete the sentences. **Answer** the questions.

1.

These shapes belong together because

_____

_____

Does [⠼] fit in the group? _____

2.

These shapes belong together because

_____

_____

Does ◯ fit in the group? _____

3.

These shapes belong together because

_____

_____

Does [∷] fit in the group? _____

4.

These shapes belong together because

_____

_____

Does ◇ fit in the group? _____

Bonus Box: For each group above, add a different shape that belongs.

Mouse Tales

Problem solving comes to life with the help of props and poetry!

Purpose: To use the act-it-out strategy to solve story problems

Students will do the following:

- use mouse props to act out story problems
- solve story problems

Materials for each student:

- copy of page 136
- crayons
- scissors
- small resealable plastic bag to store the reproducible mouse props (optional)
- pencil

Vocabulary to review:

- act it out
- solve

Extension activities to use after the reproducible:

- If your students are hungry for more problem solving, serve up additional math practice with these tempting manipulatives! Give each student a construction paper elephant cutout and several shelled peanuts. Provide a related story problem, such as "Ella the elephant has eight peanuts. She gives four peanuts to her baby. How many peanuts does Ella have left?" Guide the children to use the peanuts to solve the problem. After revealing the answer, challenge students with additional elephant-themed problems. For more fun with the act-it-out strategy, try using candy corn with crow cutouts or goldfish-shaped crackers with paper ponds. No doubt your students will savor this mouthwatering approach to problem solving!

- Set the stage for math success! In advance, place a variety of costume items—such as hats, scarves, and Halloween masks—in a large box. To begin, invite a desired number of students to the front of the class. Have each youngster don a costume. Next, provide an appropriate story problem. Ask the costumed youngsters to act out the problem; then challenge the seated students to identify the answer. After the answer is confirmed, give the young actors a round of applause. Invite different students to take their places. Continue the process until every child has had a turn to be in the spotlight. This math activity is sure to be a hit, so don't be surprised if students request a repeat performance!

Mouse Tales

Color and **cut** out the mice below.
Fold the tabs.
Use the mice to solve the problems.

1. Five little mice sit on a gate. One more joins them, a little late. Now how many mice sit on the gate? _____	2. Two hungry mice eat yellow cheese. Three smart mice write the ABCs. How many mice are there, if you please? _____
3. Six brave mice climb up a tall clock. Two fell off when it said, "Tick-tock." How many mice are still on the clock? _____	4. Four silly mice wanted to play. Mommy Mouse said just two could stay. How many mice did she send away? _____
5. Five hot mice swim in the cool lake. Three get out to eat chocolate cake. How many mice are still in the lake? _____	6. Four happy mice play some kickball. Two other mice shop at the mall. Now how many mice are there in all? _____

Bonus Box: On the back of this sheet, write a number sentence for problem 6.

Which Team?

No doubt your students will be game for solving this team mix-up!

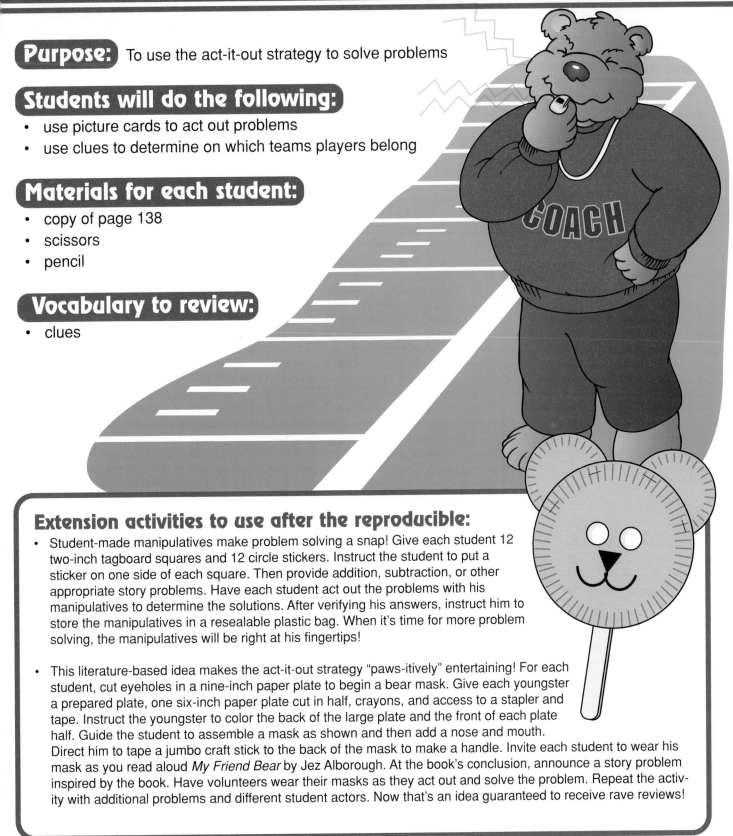

Purpose: To use the act-it-out strategy to solve problems

Students will do the following:
- use picture cards to act out problems
- use clues to determine on which teams players belong

Materials for each student:
- copy of page 138
- scissors
- pencil

Vocabulary to review:
- clues

Extension activities to use after the reproducible:

- Student-made manipulatives make problem solving a snap! Give each student 12 two-inch tagboard squares and 12 circle stickers. Instruct the student to put a sticker on one side of each square. Then provide addition, subtraction, or other appropriate story problems. Have each student act out the problems with his manipulatives to determine the solutions. After verifying his answers, instruct him to store the manipulatives in a resealable plastic bag. When it's time for more problem solving, the manipulatives will be right at his fingertips!

- This literature-based idea makes the act-it-out strategy "paws-itively" entertaining! For each student, cut eyeholes in a nine-inch paper plate to begin a bear mask. Give each youngster a prepared plate, one six-inch paper plate cut in half, crayons, and access to a stapler and tape. Instruct the youngster to color the back of the large plate and the front of each plate half. Guide the student to assemble a mask as shown and then add a nose and mouth. Direct him to tape a jumbo craft stick to the back of the mask to make a handle. Invite each student to wear his mask as you read aloud *My Friend Bear* by Jez Alborough. At the book's conclusion, announce a story problem inspired by the book. Have volunteers wear their masks as they act out and solve the problem. Repeat the activity with additional problems and different student actors. Now that's an idea guaranteed to receive rave reviews!

Which Team?

Cut out the shirts.
Read the clues and team lists.
Use the cutouts.
Write each name on the correct list.

Team Lists

Cubs (team shirt: red)

_____

_____

Black Bears (team shirt: blue)

_____

_____

Grizzlies (team shirt: green)

_____

_____

Clues

1. Jon and Ann play for the Black Bears.
2. Sue wears a green shirt.
3. Chin is not on Jon's or Sue's team.
4. Sam wears a red shirt.
5. Lucy, Bill, and Ann are on the same team.
6. Joy does not wear a red or a blue shirt.

Bonus Box: How many more players do the Grizzlies need to have the same number of players as the Black Bears? Write your answer on the back of this sheet.

Jon

Sue

Chin

Lucy

Bill

Joy

Ann

Sam

Down on the Farm

Draw on your youngsters' problem-solving skills to complete a barnyard scene!

Purpose: To use the draw-a-picture strategy to solve story problems

Students will do the following:

- draw animals to complete a barnyard scene
- use pictures to solve problems

Materials for each student:

- copy of page 140
- 12" x 18" sheet of white construction paper
- crayons
- scissors
- glue
- pencil

Vocabulary to review:

- solve

Extension activities to use after the reproducible:

- Put a little enchantment into problem solving! Attach a construction paper star topper to each of a class supply of new pencils. Explain that the class will pretend that the pencils are magic math wands. With a great deal of fanfare, present one to each youngster along with a sheet of drawing paper. Have each student illustrate a castle on the left side of the paper, leaving the right side blank for additional illustrations. Next, dictate a fairy tale–themed math problem, such as "There are five toads. The fairy godmother changes three of them into rabbits. How many are still toads?" After each youngster uses the draw-a-picture strategy to solve the problem, discuss the answer as a class. Continue with additional problems as desired. Abracadabra—problem solving is a snap!

- Believe it or not, the playground is a perfect source for story problems! Before a selected recess, ask students to pay particular attention to their playtime activities, explaining that the recess will be the inspiration for a class math book. After recess, pair students. On provided paper, have each student write a recess-related story problem. Then ask him to trade his paper with his partner. Instruct each youngster to draw a picture to solve his partner's problem and then return the paper to be checked. After any needed corrections are made, bind students' completed work into a class book titled "Playground Math."

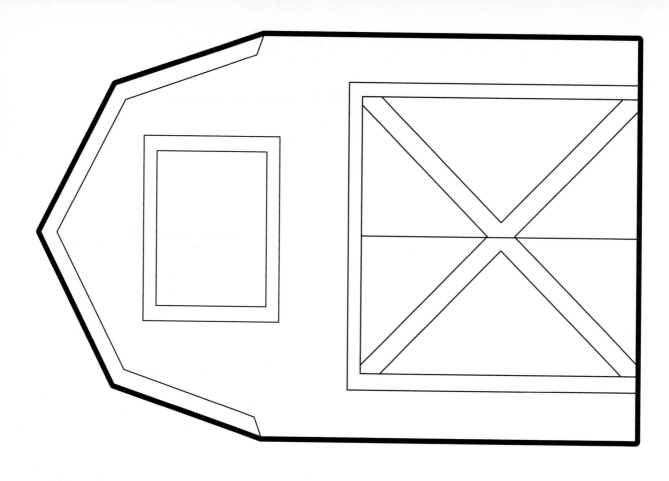

Name _____

Down on the Farm

Cut out the barn. **Glue** it on a sheet of paper.
Complete the farm picture to solve the problems.
Write the answers.

1. There are 3 chickens on the barn roof. How many legs do they have in all? _____

2. The farmer has 4 cats. He sees 2 of the cats sitting in the barn window. How many cats are not in the window? _____

3. The hens are standing in 2 rows. There are 3 hens in each row. How many hens are there in all? _____

4. The farmer has 6 pigs. He feeds each pig 2 buckets of corn. How many buckets does he feed the pigs in all? _____

Bonus Box: If there are 16 legs, how many horses would there be? Draw a picture on the back of this sheet to solve the problem. Write the answer in a complete sentence.

Camp Math-and-More

Head to the great outdoors for picture-perfect problem-solving practice!

Purpose: To use the draw-a-picture strategy to solve problems

Students will do the following:

- complete pictures to represent given problems
- use pictures to solve story problems

Materials for each student:

- copy of page 142
- pencil

Vocabulary to review:

- solve
- in all

Extension activities to use after the reproducible:

- When it comes to kid-pleasing problem-solving strategies, drawing can't be beat! Remind students that drawing pictures is a helpful problem-solving strategy. Point out that it is not necessary to create perfect likenesses, though. A quick doodle or simple representation is all that is usually needed! To provide practice using drawings as a math tool, give each student a small notepad or booklet. Invite the youngster to personalize the front cover as desired. Each day, pose a different math word problem. Have each youngster turn to his first blank page, draw a picture that represents the problem, and write the solution. Arrange for each youngster to share his work with a partner; then discuss the answer as a class.

- This appetizing idea is a surefire way to show how handy problem solving can be! Tell your students that you are planning to provide a class snack of cheese and crackers but that first you need help figuring out how many crackers to buy. Explain that each student will get three (or another specified number of) crackers. Next, divide students into small groups. Give each group a sheet of paper and have the students sketch pictures to determine how many crackers are needed for their group. Help the groups determine a class total, and follow up by serving the snack as planned. Mmmm! Math really does make a difference!

Camp Math-and-More

Read each problem.
Complete the picture to solve it.
Write the answer.

---

1. There are 2 canoes.
   Three campers ride in each
   canoe.
   How many campers are
   there? _____

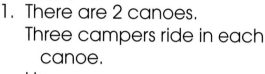

---

2. Two campers can sleep in 1
   tent.
   How many tents do 6 campers
   need? _____

---

3. Rex and Rita each toast 2
   marshmallows.
   Rich toasts 3 marshmallows.
   How many marshmallows do
   they toast in all? _____

---

4. Rex caught 5 fish.
   Rich caught 1 more fish than
   Rex.
   How many fish did they catch
   in all? _____

Bonus Box: There are 6 campers. Each camper has 3 postcards. How many
postcards do the campers have in all? On the back of this sheet, draw a picture
to solve the problem. Write the answer.

Snack Stand Savings

Count on patterns to make this activity a profitable investment in problem solving!

Purpose: To use patterns to solve problems

Students will do the following:

- determine and continue patterns
- use patterns to solve problems
- describe patterns

Materials for each student:

- copy of page 144
- pencil

Vocabulary to review:

- table
- pattern

Days	Lemonade	Cookies
Monday	5¢	5¢
Tuesday	10¢	10¢
...sday	5¢	15¢
...day	10¢	...
...ay	5¢	25...

Extension activities to use after the reproducible:

- This versatile idea provides problem-solving practice in a jiffy! In advance, prepare a blank tagboard table like the one shown. Label the first column and number the spaces as indicated. Laminate the table and then display it. Choose a desired problem-solving topic, such as the number of pizzas sold in a week or how many times a youngster jumps rope on a particular day. Label the second column of the table accordingly. Use a wipe-off marker to establish a pattern; then pose a related problem to students. Invite volunteers to identify and complete the pattern. After the class successfully uses the pattern to solve the problem, wipe off the table to prepare for another brain-boosting challenge!

Days	Pizzas
1	2
2	4
3	6
4	8
5	
6	
7	

- Here's a sweet problem! Tell students that you will give each of them four jelly beans (or a specified number of another bite-size treat). To determine how many jelly beans you need, divide students into small groups. Give each group a length of paper. Have each group make a table that indicates the total number of jelly beans needed for the entire class. After each group completes its table, display students' work. Encourage students to describe the growing pattern displayed and to discuss any variations in the groups' problem-solving strategies. Confirm the answer and then celebrate a job well done with the much-anticipated class treat!

Snack Stand Savings

Larry and Kaila sell lemonade and cookies.
The tables show how much money they have made this week.
Look at the patterns.
Complete the tables.

	Kaila's Cookies			
Monday	Tuesday	Wednesday	Thursday	Friday
5¢	10¢	15¢		

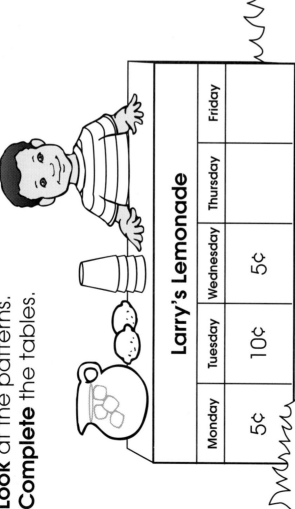

	Larry's Lemonade			
Monday	Tuesday	Wednesday	Thursday	Friday
5¢	10¢	5¢		

1. If their sales follow the patterns above, who will make more money on Friday: Larry or Kaila? _____ How much more? _____

2. Write a sentence that tells about each pattern above.

   Larry's pattern: _____

   Kaila's pattern: _____

Bonus Box: On the back of this sheet, make a different table that shows how much money Larry will make on Saturday and Sunday if the pattern continues.

Shoppers' Paradise!

Shopping for a great list-making activity? Check this out!

Purpose: To solve problems by making lists

Students will do the following:

- organize groups of items into lists
- list all possible combinations of a group of items
- use reasoning skills

Materials for each student:

- copy of page 146
- pencil
- crayons

Vocabulary to review:

- list
- label

Extension activities to use after the reproducible:

- Use this simple whole-group activity to make a list and check it twice! On the chalkboard, list three of the day's activities, such as reading, snack, and writing. Explain to students that they need to do all three activities, but the class will decide in which order to complete them. To begin the decision-making process, write one possible sequence on the chalkboard. Enlist students' help to write the remaining possibilities. Poll the class to determine the students' favorite sequence. Then use the sequence with the greatest number of votes to structure the day's activities!

- Serve up list-making practice with this hands-on activity! Place grocery store circulars, paper, scissors, glue, and crayons at a center. To use the center, have a student imagine that he will serve three different foods at dinnertime and he needs to decide the order in which to do so. The student divides his paper into six equal sections. He cuts out three foods from a circular. Next, the youngster arranges the pictures in a sequence of his choice on a work surface. He illustrates the sequence in the first section of his paper. The youngster rearranges the pictures and repeats the process until he has illustrated six different sequences. Then, on another sheet of paper, he glues the pictures to show his favorite sequence. Dinner is served!

Shoppers' Paradise!

Read. Follow the directions.

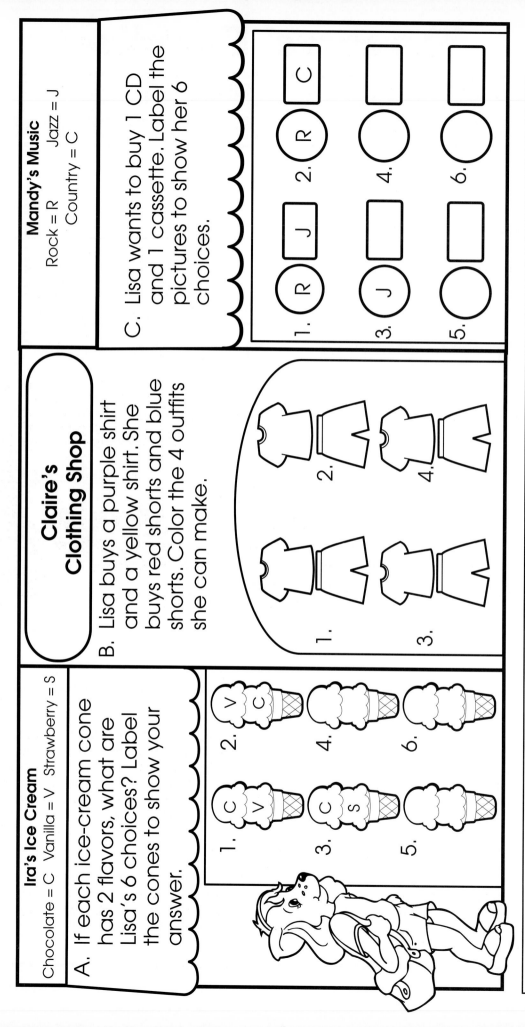

Ira's Ice Cream

Chocolate = C   Vanilla = V   Strawberry = S

A. If each ice-cream cone has 2 flavors, what are Lisa's 6 choices? Label the cones to show your answer.

Claire's Clothing Shop

B. Lisa buys a purple shirt and a yellow shirt. She buys red shorts and blue shorts. Color the 4 outfits she can make.

Mandy's Music

Rock = R   Jazz = J
Country = C

C. Lisa wants to buy 1 CD and 1 cassette. Label the pictures to show her 6 choices.

Bonus Box: Shopping made Lisa hungry! She can have a hot dog or hamburger. She can have fries or onion rings with it. On the back of this sheet, use crayons to show the 4 different meals she can have.

©2001 The Education Center, Inc. • *Math Skills Workout* • TEC3225 • Key p. 174

Count on Cookies!

This batch of problem-solving fun is a real treat!

Purpose: To use a table to solve problems

Students will do the following:

- complete a table
- use a table to solve problems

Materials for each student:

- copy of page 148
- pencil
- crayons

Vocabulary to review:

- table

Extension activities to use after the reproducible:

- If your students crave more practice using tables, this small-group follow-up is sure to hit the spot! Give each group a 12" x 18" sheet of white paper. Provide access to crayons, glue, scissors, and a supply of construction paper. Tell students that Paws has asked her friend Patches to help her make cookies. In the time that it takes Paws to make two cookies, Patches makes three. Challenge each group to determine how many cookies Patches will make by the time Paws makes eight cookies *(12)*. To do so, each group makes and labels on its paper a two-row table with eight spaces. To complete the table, the group members make the appropriate number of construction paper cookies for each space and then glue them in place. Display each group's table. Discuss the pattern shown and check students' answers.

- Which school subject is tops among your students? Find out with this table-making idea! To prepare, photocopy a small school photo of each student. On a strip of bulletin board paper, make a table that has a column heading for each school subject. Ask students to predict what subject is the class favorite. Next, post the table and have each youngster glue his photocopied photo in the column that reflects his own preference. Then guide students to use the table to check their predictions.

Name _____

Count on Cookies!

Paws is planning a party.
She wants to give 2 cookies to each guest.
How many cookies does she need?
Complete the table to find out.

Guests	1	2	3	4	5	6
Cookies	🍪🍪	🍪🍪🍪🍪				

Look at the table. **Answer** the questions.

1. How many cookies does Paws need for 4 guests? _____

2. How many cookies does Paws need for 6 guests? _____

3. Paws has baked 6 cookies. If 5 guests come to the party, how many more cookies does she need? _____

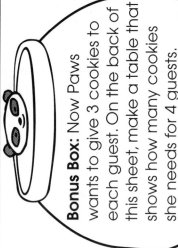

Bonus Box: Now Paws wants to give 3 cookies to each guest. On the back of this sheet, make a table that shows how many cookies she needs for 4 guests.

©2001 The Education Center, Inc. • *Math Skills Workout* • TEC3225 • Key p. 174

Doughnut Delights

Sweeten problem solving with this mouthwatering activity!

Purpose: To use the make-a-table strategy to solve problems

Students will do the following:

- complete tables
- use tables to solve problems

Materials for each student:

- copy of page 150
- pencil

Vocabulary to review:

- table

Extension activities to use after the reproducible:

- Simplify math-time preparation with these reusable tables! On a sheet of duplicating paper, draw a blank table with two rows. Make one copy for every two students. Pair students. Give each twosome a copy of the table, a wipe-off marker, a facial tissue, two light-colored crayons, and a top-loading, plastic sheet protector. The young-sters color each row of the table a different color for easy reference. Then they insert the table into the sheet protector. To solve a given story problem, the students use the marker to complete the table. They record their answer as directed and then erase the table to prepare it for another problem.

- This problem-solving idea is one for the books! Prepare an 8" x 24" tagboard table like the one shown. Program the front of an envelope with a selected book title and a story-related problem. Inside a construction paper folder, make a completed table that can be used to check the answers. Next, copy each table heading on a separate 3" x 5" index card. Copy each value from the table on a separate index card half. Tuck the cards in the envelope. Place the envelope, table, and answer key at a center. At the conclusion of the featured book, a student reads the problem, arranges the cards on the prepared table to solve the problem, and then opens the folder to check his work. Now that's a math center with a happy ending!

Minutes	1	2	3	4	5
Bricks	5	10			

Answer Key

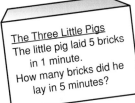

The Three Little Pigs
The little pig laid 5 bricks in 1 minute.
How many bricks did he lay in 5 minutes?

Doughnut Delights

Read each problem.
Complete the table.
Write the answer on the line.

1. Baker Bob makes 2 boxes of doughnuts each hour.
   How many boxes of doughnuts does he make in 5 hours? _____

Hours	1	2	3	4	5
Boxes of Doughnuts	2	4			

2. Each doughnut costs 10¢.
   How much do 5 doughnuts cost? _____

Doughnuts	1	2	3		
Cost	10¢	20¢			

3. A doughnut machine makes 5 doughnuts every 2 minutes.
   How many minutes does it take to make 20 doughnuts? _____

Minutes	2	4	6		
Doughnuts	5	10	15		

Bonus Box: Think about the table in problem 2. How many doughnuts could you buy with 70¢? Write the answer on the back of this sheet.

©2001 The Education Center, Inc. • *Math Skills Workout* • TEC3225 • Key p. 174

Crayon Confusion

Brighten up problem-solving practice with the guess-and-check strategy!

Purpose: To solve problems using the guess-and-check strategy

Students will do the following:
- use manipulatives to solve problems
- check guesses by adding money amounts

Materials for each student:
- copy of page 152
- pencil
- crayons
- scissors

Vocabulary to review:
- guess and check
- price

Extension activities to use after the reproducible:

- This idea sharpens students' problem-solving skills by the numbers! In advance, number two sets of blank cards 1–5. Place two randomly selected cards in a pocket chart so that the numbers are concealed. Provide two clues about the concealed numbers, such as "The sum of the numbers is seven. One number is three more than the other." Model how to manipulate cubes to try various number combinations in order to identify the described numbers. Then flip the cards to reveal the answer. Next, provide each student with ten cubes. Present additional problems with different number pairs for students to solve as demonstrated. You can be sure that improved thinking skills will be in the cards!

- Strengthen math vocabularies with this guess-and-check activity! Secretly choose a familiar math word and then draw a blank for each letter of the word on the chalkboard. Next, ask students to guess the word. Write the guesses on the board without revealing the correct word. After students have made several guesses, guide them to eliminate words from the list that do not have the correct number of letters. To help students confirm a correct guess or eliminate other incorrect guesses, write the first letter of the word in the corresponding blank. As necessary, provide additional letter clues one at a time as students continue the process of guessing and checking until they correctly identify the word.

Suggested Math Vocabulary		
add	subtract	more
less	sum	total
difference	equal	solve

Crayon Confusion

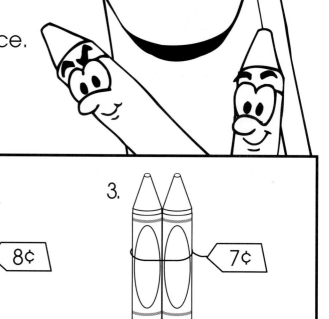

Color the crayons at the bottom of the sheet.
Cut them out.

For each set of crayons, **read** the price.
Color to match the price.
Use the cutouts to help you.

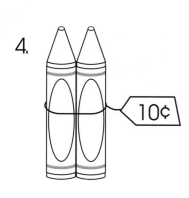

1. 5¢

2. 8¢

3. 7¢

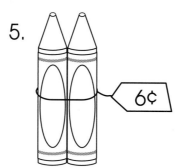

4. 10¢

5. 6¢

6. 6¢

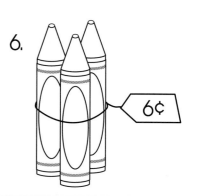

Bonus Box: Look at number 3. If there were 3 crayons, what colors would they be? On the back of this sheet, write and illustrate your answer.

©2001 The Education Center, Inc. • *Math Skills Workout* • TEC3225 • Key p. 174

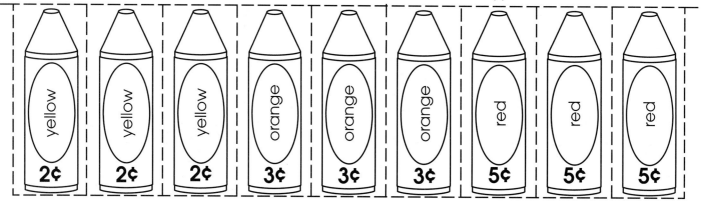

yellow 2¢ | yellow 2¢ | yellow 2¢ | orange 3¢ | orange 3¢ | orange 3¢ | red 5¢ | red 5¢ | red 5¢

Wild About Number Sentences!

This trip to the zoo provides fun-filled practice using number sentences to solve problems!

Purpose: To solve story problems by writing number sentences

Students will do the following:

- write number sentences for story problems
- use number sentences to solve story problems

Materials for each student:

- copy of page 154
- pencil

Vocabulary to review:

- number sentence
- addition
- subtraction
- solve

Extension activities to use after the reproducible:

- Try this handy tip to help students focus on key words in story problems. Have students brainstorm words that give hints about the appropriate operations to use for story problems, such as *more, left,* or *in all.* Remind students that because some story problems do not have easily identifiable key words, it is important to read problems carefully. Next, give each student a yellow crayon and a sheet of story problems. Have each student use her crayon to highlight the key words or phrases. Invite students to tell the class the words they marked and why. Continue with the remaining problems in a like manner; then instruct each youngster to solve them. What a bright way to help students think carefully about story problems!

- Personalize problem solving with this classy display! For each student, fold a 5" x 7" index card in half and program the outside of the card with a different story problem. Provide each student with a prepared card, two 2½-inch half circles, one six-inch circle, and a sentence strip. Inside the card, have him write the operation he thinks he should use to solve the problem, his reasoning, and the solution. Then have him make a self-likeness and staple the card to it as illustrated. Display students' completed work on a bulletin board titled "The 'Write' Operation."

Wild About Number Sentences!

Read the story problems.
Write the number sentence
for each problem.

ZOO

A.  splashes the water
6 times.
She splashes 3 more times.
How many times does she
splash in all?

☐ ◯ ☐ = ☐

B. has 11 fish.

He hides 4 fish.
How many fish are left?

☐ ◯ ☐ = ☐

C. has 6 bananas.

She peels 2 of them.
How many bananas are left
to peel?

☐ ◯ ☐ = ☐

D. eats 7 leaves.

He eats 5 more leaves.
How many leaves does he
eat in all?

☐ ◯ ☐ = ☐

E.  runs 6 laps in the morning.

He runs 5 more laps in the
afternoon.
How many laps does he run
in all?

☐ ◯ ☐ = ☐

F. sees 10 boys at the zoo.

She sees 3 girls.
How many more boys than
girls does she see?

☐ ◯ ☐ = ☐

Bonus Box: Choose an animal from above. On the back of this sheet, write a story
problem about it. Have a friend write a number sentence to solve the problem.

Game for Problem Solving

Put an entertaining spin on problem solving with this review activity!

Purpose: To select and use appropriate problem-solving strategies

Students will do the following:

- choose one of the following strategies to solve a given problem: draw a picture, make a list, make a table, or write a number sentence
- solve story problems

Materials for each student:

- copy of page 156
- pencil
- sheet of blank paper to provide extra problem-solving space, if needed

Vocabulary to review:

- strategy
- solve
- draw a picture
- make a list
- make a table
- write a number sentence

Extension activities to use after the reproducible:

- Problem solving is a snap when students have the tools of the trade at their fingertips! Give each youngster a small gift box and a list of problem-solving strategies. Invite her to personalize the box, and have her store the list inside it. Arrange for her to stock her box with materials such as a small resealable plastic bag of counters, a booklet for making lists and writing solutions, and a ruler for making tables. Have the student store the resulting math toolbox in her desk for easy access. To help the class make a smooth transition to math time, post a story problem as students settle in. Students will have everything they need to get right to work, and no precious instructional time will be lost distributing materials!

- This problem-solving idea is beyond compare! Program a class supply of blank cards with story problems (or have each student write an original story problem). Randomly distribute the cards and give each student a sheet of unlined paper. Each youngster divides his paper in half. On each half, he uses a different strategy to solve the problem, such as drawing a picture or writing a number sentence. On the back of the paper, the youngster explains which strategy was easier to use and why. Invite students to share their explanations with the class. Students are sure to see that different strategies are useful in different ways!

Game for Problem Solving

Read each problem.
Circle to show the strategy you will use.
Solve the problem in the empty box.
Write the answer on the line.

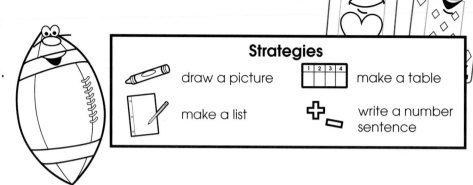

Strategies

draw a picture   make a table

make a list   write a number sentence

---

1. Jane wants to play tag, baseball, and cards. She cannot decide the order in which to play the games. How many ways can she play them? _____

2. Nick makes 3 touchdowns. Sally makes 4 touchdowns. How many touchdowns do they make in all? _____

3. There are 7 children playing marbles. Each child has 2 marbles. How many marbles are there in all? _____

4. The team makes 2 home runs on Monday. It makes 4 home runs on Tuesday. If the team keeps this pattern, how many home runs will it make on Saturday? _____

Bonus Box: On the back of this sheet, write a number sentence. Then ask a friend to write a story problem that matches.

The Sweet Smell of Success

Students' problem-solving skills are sure to bloom with this "scent-sational" activity!

Purpose: To select and use appropriate problem-solving strategies

Students will do the following:

- choose strategies to solve problems
- solve problems

Materials for each student:

- copy of page 158
- pencil
- crayons
- sheet of blank paper to provide extra problem-solving space, if needed

Vocabulary to review:

- solve
- strategy
- pattern
- number sentence
- table

Extension activities to use after the reproducible:

- The strategy for this problem-solving activity is clear—get every student actively involved! Divide an 8¹/₂" x 11" sheet of paper into quarters. Program each quarter with a different problem-solving strategy. Give each student a copy of the sheet and have him cut it into quarters to make cards. Provide a story problem that could be solved with one of the featured strategies. Have each student decide which strategy is the most appropriate and then hold up the corresponding card. Invite a student who holds the correct card to explain his reasoning to the class. Have all the students return the cards to their desktops. Repeat the activity a desired number of times.

- This class activity results in a handy reminder of problem-solving strategies! To make a poster for each strategy, draw a one-inch border along the edges of a separate 12" x 18" sheet of white paper. Title the paper with the strategy and write a student-generated problem that can be solved with it. Assign a small group to each poster. (If you have a large number of students, you may want to prepare multiple posters for selected strategies.) Have the youngsters use the strategy to solve the problem on the poster. After the students embellish the border, display each group's poster.

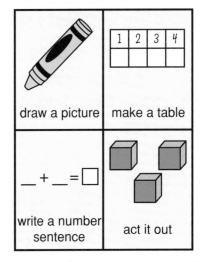

The Sweet Smell of Success

Solve each problem.
Write the answer.
For each problem you solve,
    color one petal of Skunk's flower.

Remember to use the best strategy!

---

1. There are 5 birds. Each bird lays 2 eggs. How many eggs are there in all? _____

2. Rabbit eats 2 carrots for breakfast and 2 carrots for lunch. She eats 3 carrots for dinner. How many carrots does she eat in all? _____

3. Read the clues. Color the correct flower below.

   Clues
   a. It has 2 leaves.
   b. It does not have pointed petals.
   c. It has an even number of petals.

4. Skunk picks 1 flower on Monday. He picks 3 flowers on Tuesday. He picks 5 flowers on Wednesday. If he continues this pattern, how many flowers will he pick on Friday? _____

Bonus Box: On the back of this sheet, write how you solved number 4.

Hundred Chart

1	2	3	4	5	6	7	8	9	10
11	12	13	14	15	16	17	18	19	20
21	22	23	24	25	26	27	28	29	30
31	32	33	34	35	36	37	38	39	40
41	42	43	44	45	46	47	48	49	50
51	52	53	54	55	56	57	58	59	60
61	62	63	64	65	66	67	68	69	70
71	72	73	74	75	76	77	78	79	80
81	82	83	84	85	86	87	88	89	90
91	92	93	94	95	96	97	98	99	100

Place-Value Mat

©2001 The Education Center, Inc. • *Math Skills Workout* • TEC3225

Note to the teacher: Use this place-value mat with the extension ideas on page 13. To use a copy of the mat, a student places
one manipulative on a separate popcorn box to represent each ten. He places one manipulative on a separate popcorn piece
to represent each one.

Math Airways Ticket

Name _____
(student name)

Flight Information	**Flight Check**

Flight Information

1. _____ – _____ = _____

2. _____ – _____ = _____

3. _____ – _____ = _____

4. _____ – _____ = _____

5. _____ – _____ = _____

Flight Check

1. _____ + _____ = _____

2. _____ + _____ = _____

3. _____ + _____ = _____

4. _____ + _____ = _____

5. _____ + _____ = _____

Frog Counters
Use with the first extension activity on page 39.

Patterns

Use the inch ruler with "By Leaps and Bounds!" on pages 59–60.
Use the centimeter ruler with "Leafy Lengths" on pages 61–62.

inch ruler

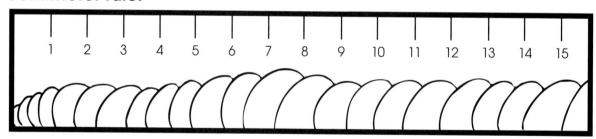

centimeter ruler

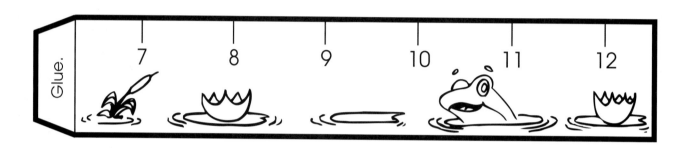

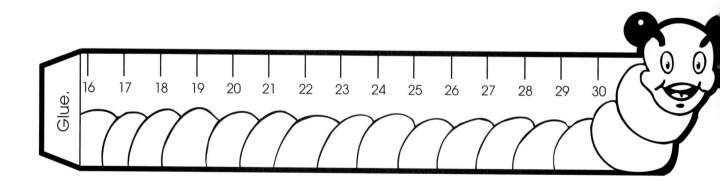

Note to the teacher: To prepare a customary and a metric ruler, make a copy of this page. Carefully cut along the bold lines.
Glue together each ruler where indicated. Allow the glue to dry.

clock face

clock hands

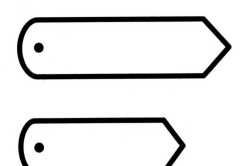

Note to the teacher: Give each student a tagboard copy of this page. Have the youngster color the clock hands and face, leaving the numbers visible. Direct her to cut along the bold lines. Then help her use a brad to secure the clock hands to the clock face where indicated.

Patterns

Use with selected reproducible and extension activities on pages 89–94.

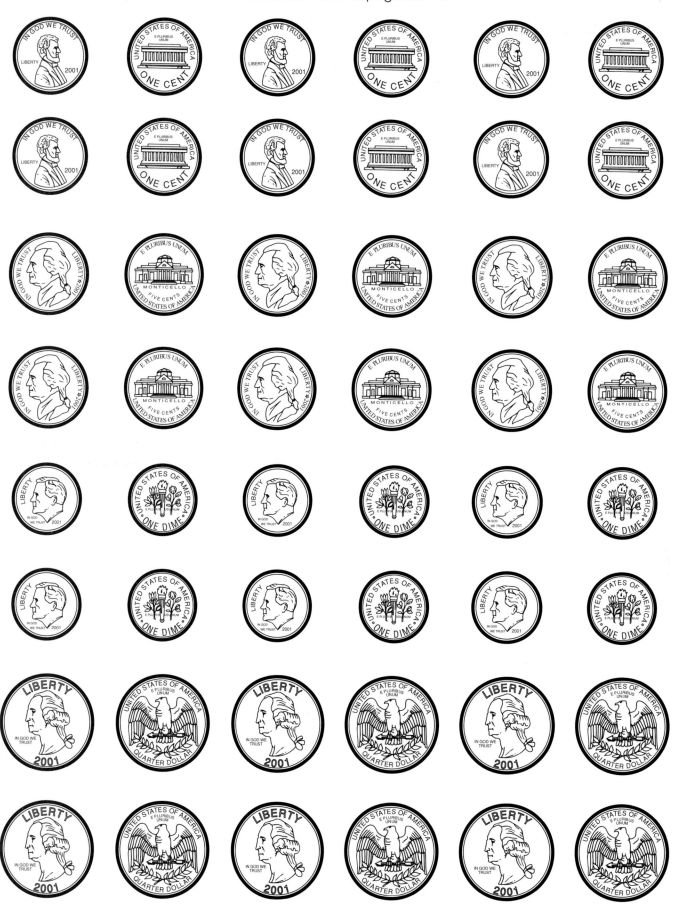

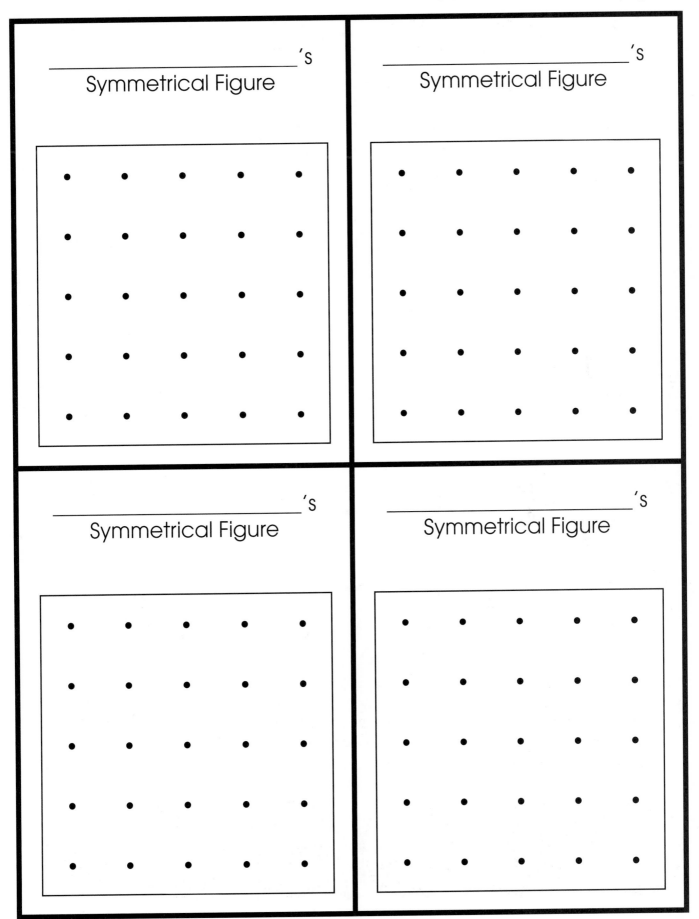

_____'s
Symmetrical Figure

_____'s
Symmetrical Figure

_____'s
Symmetrical Figure

_____'s
Symmetrical Figure

Patterns
Use the spinner wheel with the second extension activity on page 129 and the
cards with the activity on page 130.

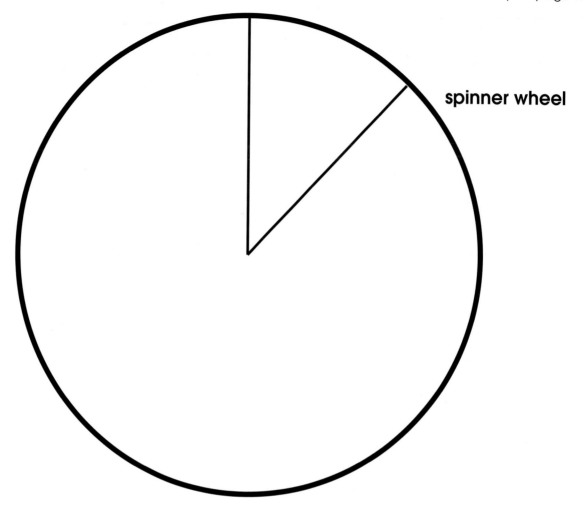

spinner wheel

cards

Answer Keys

Page 6

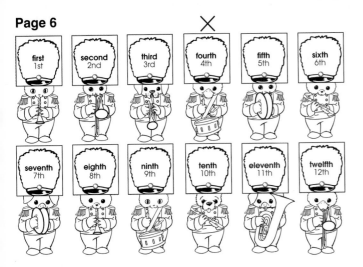

Bonus Box: The duck is playing a drum.

Page 8

1. 56, <u>57</u>, <u>58</u>, 59, <u>60</u>, 61, <u>62</u>, <u>63</u> (green)
2. 11, 12, <u>13</u>, <u>14</u>, <u>15</u>, 16, 17, <u>18</u> (brown)
3. <u>38</u>, 39, <u>40</u>, 41, <u>42</u>, <u>43</u>, 44, <u>45</u> (brown)
4. 91, <u>92</u>, <u>93</u>, <u>94</u>, 95, <u>96</u>, 97, <u>98</u> (green)
5. 79, <u>80</u>, <u>81</u>, <u>82</u>, 83, <u>84</u>, <u>85</u>, <u>86</u> (green)
6. <u>72</u>, 73, <u>74</u>, 75, <u>76</u>, <u>77</u>, <u>78</u>, 79 (green)

Bonus Box: 19, 20, 21, 22, 23, 24, 25, 26, 27, 28

Page 10

1. 86, 87, <u>88</u>, <u>89</u>, 90, <u>91</u>, <u>92</u>, 93, <u>94</u>
2. <u>56</u>, 55, <u>54</u>, <u>53</u>, 52, <u>51</u>
3. 74, <u>75</u>, 76, <u>77</u>, <u>78</u>, <u>79</u>, 80
4. 71, <u>70</u>, 69, 68, <u>67</u>, <u>66</u>

The following numbers should be circled: 94, 56, 80, 71.
The following numbers should be crossed out: 86, 51, 74, 66.

Bonus Box: 57, 60, 75, 82, 86, 93, 100

Page 12

a. 4 (red)
b. 5 (blue)
c. 7 (blue)
d. 8 (red)
e. 1 (blue)
f. 3 (blue)
g. 2 (red)
h. 6 (red)

Bonus Box: 1 (blue), 2 (red), 3 (blue), 4 (red), 5 (blue), 6 (red), 7 (blue), 8 (red), 9 (blue), 10 (red). Sentences will vary but should indicate that there is a pattern.

Page 14

a. 12
b. 33
c. 50
d. 27
e. 41
f. 19

Bonus Box: Each student should have drawn 2 popcorn boxes and 5 pieces of popcorn. There are 2 tens and 5 ones.

Page 16

1. 1 ten, 3 ones; 13
2. 2 tens, 0 ones; 20
3. 2 tens, 2 ones; 22
4. 3 tens, 2 ones; 32

Bonus Box: Drawings will vary but should show 2 sets of 10 fish and be labeled "20."

Page 18

1. 4
2. 5
3. 7
4. 7
5. 6

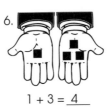 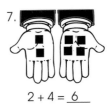 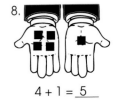

6. 1 + 3 = <u>4</u>   7. 2 + 4 = <u>6</u>   8. 4 + 1 = <u>5</u>

Bonus Box: 3 + 3 = 6

Page 20

a. 3 + 3 = 6
b. 2 + 3 = 5
c. 2 + 2 = 4
d. 5 + 1 = 6
e. 4 + 0 = 4
f. 1 + 2 = 3

Bonus Box: 4 + 4 = 8

Page 22

1. 7
2. 8
3. 10
4. 8
5. 6
6. 5
7. 9
8. 8
9. 10
10. 6
11. 7
12. 9

Bonus Box: 3 + 7 = 10. Students should have drawn pictures of space rocks to correspond with the number sentence.

Page 24

a. 9
b. 10 (K)
c. 7
d. 8
e. 7
f. 9
g. 10 (K)
h. 6
i. 6
j. 9

Bonus Box: The following mittens should be outlined in green: b, d, g, h, i. The following mittens should be outlined in purple: a, c, e, f, j.

167

Page 26

a. 10
b. 12 (brown)
c. 11
d. 9
e. 11
f. 12 (brown)
g. 12 (brown)
h. 10
i. 12 (brown)

Bonus Box: 2 + 9 = 11. Clyde sells 11 ice-cream treats in all.

Page 28

a. 4
b. 8
c. 6
d. 10
e. 2
f. 6
g. 12
h. 4
i. 10
j. 4
k. 2
l. 6
m. 6, 12
n. 3, 6
o. 5, 5, 10

Bonus Box: Answers will vary. Accept any reasonable responses.

Page 30

5 + 7 = 12
7 + 5 = 12
12 − 5 = 7
12 − 7 = 5

1 + 6 = 7
6 + 1 = 7
7 − 1 = 6
7 − 6 = 1

3 + 6 = 9
6 + 3 = 9
9 − 3 = 6
9 − 6 = 3

8 + 3 = 11
3 + 8 = 11
11 − 3 = 8
11 − 8 = 3

Bonus Box: 4 + 6 = 10, 6 + 4 = 10, 10 − 4 = 6, 10 − 6 = 4

Page 32

1. 5
2. 8
3. 12
4. 11
5. 12
6. 8
7. 9
8. 11
9. 10

Bonus Box: Accept any 2 of the following answers:
8 + 2 + 1 = 11, 8 + 1 + 2 = 11, 2 + 8 + 1 = 11,
2 + 1 + 8 = 11, 1 + 8 + 2 = 11, 1 + 2 + 8 = 11.

Page 34

Bonus Box: 3 + 2 = 5 or 2 + 3 = 5. The student should have drawn a corresponding picture.

Page 36

1. See 5 in all. Eat 1. Leave 4.	2. See 8 in all. Eat 2. Leave 6.	3. See 4 in all. Eat 1. Leave 3.
5 − 1 = 4	8 − 2 = 6	4 − 1 = 3
4. See 7 in all. Eat 2. Leave 5.	5. See 6 in all. Eat 0. Leave 6.	
7 − 2 = 5	6 − 0 = 6	
6. See 7 in all. Eat 3. Leave 4.	7. See 6 in all. Eat 1. Leave 5.	
7 − 3 = 4	6 − 1 = 5	

Bonus Box: Answers will vary. Accept any reasonable responses.

Page 38

1. 8
2. 4
3. 4
4. 2
5. 6
6. 5
7. 5
8. 1
9. 9
10. 2
11. 6
12. 1
13. 7
14. 7
15. 2
16. 6
17. 8

Bonus Box: 20, 19, 18, 17, 16, 15, 14, 13, 12, 11, 10, 9, 8, 7, 6, 5, 4, 3, 2, 1

Page 40

1. 3
2. 6
3. 2
4. 5
5. 10
6. 4
7. 8
8. 7
9. 1
10. 0

Zippy likes soccer the most because he gets a kick out of it!
Bonus Box: 10 − 8 = 2

Page 42

a. 4
b. 4
c. 6
d. 2
e. 1
f. 1
g. 7
h. 3
i. 3
j. 3

The clouds with the following problems should be outlined in blue: a, b, e, f, i, and j.
The clouds with the following problems should be outlined in black: c, d, g, and h.
Bonus Box: 7 − 4 = 3. Mr. Wing saw 3 more airplanes on Tuesday.

Page 46
1. 8
2. 6
3. 8
4. 15
5. 12
6. 20
Bonus Box: The pigs have 16 legs in all.

Page 48
1. 3
2. 4
3. 2
4. 2
Bonus Box: The student should have drawn 10 gift boxes and circled 2 groups of 5.

Page 50
1. red
2. purple
3. yellow
4. red
5. purple
6. red
7. purple
8. yellow
9. purple
10. red
11. purple
Bonus Box: The following flowers should have "$^1/_2$" written beside them: 1, 4, 6, 10.

Page 52
1. $^1/_3$
2. $^1/_4$
3. $^1/_3$
4. $^1/_2$
5. $^1/_4$
6. $^1/_2$
7. $^1/_3$
8. $^1/_4$
9. $^1/_3$
10. $^1/_2$
11. $^1/_4$
12. $^1/_4$
Bonus Box: Each student should have a drawn a circle, divided it into quarters, and labeled each part "$^1/_4$."

Page 54
1. $^1/_2$
2. $^1/_3$
3. $^1/_4$
4. $^1/_2$
5. $^1/_4$
6. $^1/_3$
7. $^1/_2$
Bonus Box: The student should have drawn a picture of 3 birds in a tree and 3 birds flying.

Page 56
1. a. 2
   b. 1
   c. $^1/_2$
2. a. 3
   b. 1
   c. $^1/_3$
3. a. 4
   b. 1
   c. $^1/_4$
4. a. 5
   b. 1
   c. $^1/_5$
Bonus Box: The student should have drawn 4 baseballs, circled 1, and written the fraction $^1/_4$.

Page 58
(All estimates will vary. The actual measurements are noted below.)
1. 2
2. 5
3. 7
4. 4
5. 3
Bonus Box: Answers will vary.

Page 60
Estimates will vary.
a. 5
b. 3
c. 2
d. 4
1. Fran
2. 2
3. 5, Freddy
Bonus Box: Drawings will vary, but each student should have drawn a 3-inch-tall house and a 5-inch-tall tree.

Page 62
a. 5
b. 3
c. 6
d. 4
e. 7
f. 5
1. Leaves a and f should be colored green.
2. Leaf b should be colored yellow.
3. A star should be drawn beside leaf e.
Bonus Box: Leaf e is two centimeters longer than leaf a. Explanations will vary.

Page 64
Inch Pup's yellow bones: pencil, book, shoe, watch
Foot Hound's brown bones: fence, driveway, house, school bus, airplane
Bonus Box: Responses will vary.

Page 66

Lee's truck: house, potatoes, desk, car
Leo's truck: crayon, ruler, feather, paper clip
Bonus Box: Answers will vary.

Page 68

1. lighter
2. heavier
3. heavier
4. lighter
5. potatoes
6. flour
7. grapes
8. potatoes
9. flour
10. flour

Bonus Box: Answers will vary.

Page 70

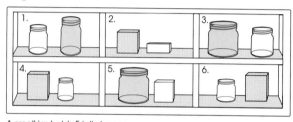

A small jar holds 5 jelly beans.
Color to show how many small jars Jake needs for each customer.

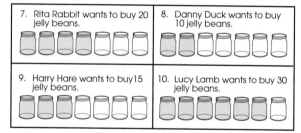

Bonus Box: A large jar holds 15 jelly beans.

Page 72

1. cool (The jacket, sweatshirt, and jeans should be colored.)
2. hot (The sandals, shorts, and bathing suit should be colored.)
3. warm (The overalls, sneakers, and shirt should be colored.)
4. cold (The hat, shirt, and gloves should be colored.)

Bonus Box: Answers will vary.

Page 74

1. less
2. more
3. less
4. more
5. less
6. less
7. more
8. less
9. more
10. less

Bonus Box: Answers will vary.

Page 76

1. Friday, Sunday
2. 4

	June					
Sunday	Monday	Tuesday	Wednesday	Thursday	Friday	Saturday
			1	2	3	4
5	6	7	8	9	10	11
12	13	14	15	16	17	18
19	20	21	22	23	24	25
26	27	28	29	30		

6. Wednesday
7. June 6

Bonus Box: January, February, March, April, May, June, July, August, September, October, November, December. The current month should be underlined. Next month should be circled.

Page 78

1. 1:00
2. 9:00
3. 3:00
4. 5:00
5. 11:00
6. 2:00
7. 6:00
8. 10:00
9. 8:00

The outlines of the following clocks should be colored: 1, 3, 4, 6, 7.

Bonus Box: Answers will vary.

Page 80

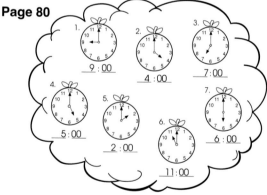

Apple number 5 should be outlined in red.
Apple number 2 should be outlined in green.
Bonus Box: The student should have drawn and labeled a clock that shows 8:00.

Page 82

1. 2:30
2. 4:30
3. 8:30
4. 1:30
5. 11:30
6. 3:30
7. 12:30
8. 9:30

Bonus Box: The student should have drawn a clock that shows 5:30. The hour hand should be blue and the minute hand should be red.

Page 84

a. 9:30
b. 7:00
c. 1:30
d. 10:00
e. 3:30
f. 4:30
g. 9:00
h. 12:30

Bonus Box: Balloon g should be colored yellow. Balloon a should be colored blue.

Page 86

1. nickels (orange)
2. quarters (blue)
3. pennies (yellow)
4. dimes (green)

Bonus Box: The student should have drawn and described any 2 of these answers: 1 dime, 2 nickels, 1 nickel and 5 pennies, 10 pennies.

Page 88

1. 10¢
2. 7¢
3. 20¢
4. 15¢
5. 13¢

Bonus Box: Accept drawings that represent any one of the following sets of coins: 20 pennies; 2 dimes; 1 dime and 2 nickels; 1 dime, 1 nickel, and 5 pennies; 1 dime and 10 pennies.

Page 90

Sammy has 45¢.

1. yes
2. no
3. yes
4. yes
5. no

Sandy has 37¢.

1. yes
2. no
3. no
4. yes
5. no

Bonus Box: Yes, Sammy has enough money because he has 45¢, and a pencil and eraser would cost 40¢ in all.

Page 92

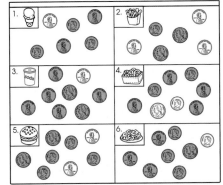

Bonus Box: It would cost 35¢ to buy french fries and a soda. Illustrations will vary.

Page 94

1. 2 dimes (orange)
2. 1 quarter, 1 nickel, 2 pennies (yellow)
3. 1 quarter, 1 penny (orange)
4. 1 dime, 1 nickel, 1 penny (red)
5. 1 quarter, 1 dime, 1 nickel (red)

Bonus Box: Answers will vary.

Page 96

Look.	Add.	Draw.	Write.
1. 10¢	2¢	10¢ 1¢ 1¢	10¢ + 2¢ = 12¢
2. 7¢	1¢	5¢ 1¢ 1¢ 1¢	7¢ + 1¢ = 8¢
3. 15¢	3¢	10¢ 5¢ 1¢ 1¢ 1¢	15¢ + 3¢ = 18¢
4. 12¢	1¢	10¢ 1¢ 1¢ 1¢	12¢ + 1¢ = 13¢
5. 25¢	2¢	25¢ 1¢ 1¢	25¢ + 2¢ = 27¢

Look.	Subtract.	Draw.	Write.
6. 12¢	2¢	10¢ ⊗ ⊗	12¢ – 2¢ = 10¢
7. 15¢	10¢	⊗ 5¢	15¢ – 10¢ = 5¢
8. 7¢	2¢	5¢ ⊗ ⊗	7¢ – 2¢ = 5¢
9. 20¢	10¢	10¢ ⊗	20¢ – 10¢ = 10¢
10. 16¢	5¢	10¢ ⊗ 1¢	16¢ – 5¢ = 11¢

Bonus Box: The student should have drawn 3 pennies and 1 quarter and written this addition sentence: 3¢ + 25¢ = 28¢.

Page 98

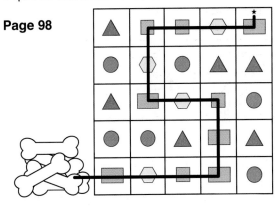

Bonus Box: The student should have drawn a triangle and written that it has 3 sides and 3 corners.

Page 100

1. red, X
2. yellow, X
3. orange
4. blue
5. green
6. orange
7. yellow, X
8. purple
9. red, X
10. blue

Bonus Box: The student should have drawn a cube-shaped object and written that it has 6 faces.

Page 102

1. red
2. orange
3. purple
4. purple
5. blue
6. orange
7. red
8. orange
9. purple
10. blue

Bonus Box: Answers will vary.

Page 104

The shapes in the following pairs should be colored alike:

1. h   5. b
2. f   6. c
3. g   7. e
4. a   8. d

Bonus Box: Answers will vary, but they should show congruent pairs of shapes.

Page 106

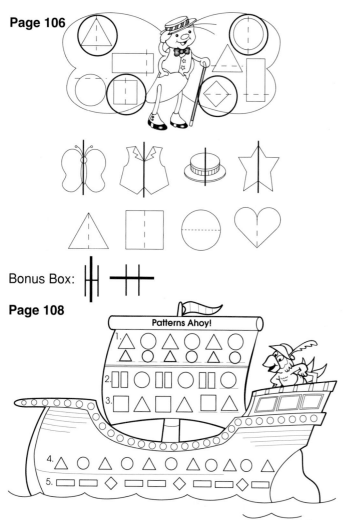

Bonus Box:

Page 108

Coloring will vary, but it should show consistency within the patterns.
Bonus Box: Answers will vary, but they should show a pattern.

Page 110

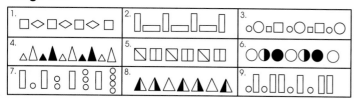

10. triangle, circle, circle, triangle, circle, circle

Bonus Box:

The description may vary.

Page 112

Coloring will vary but should reflect a pattern.

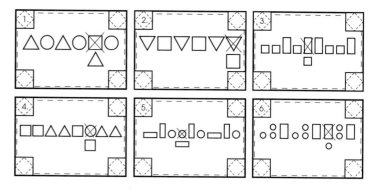

Bonus Box: Answers will vary.

Page 114

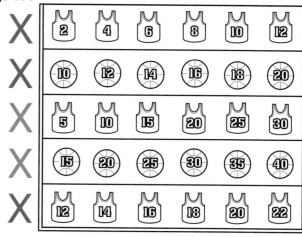

Bonus Box: Answers will vary.

Page 116

a. 5, 10, _15_, _20_, _25_ (yellow)
b. 10, 20, _30_, _40_, _50_ (orange)
c. 20, 25, _30_, _35_, _40_ (yellow)
d. 30, _40_, 50, _60_, _70_ (orange)
e. 60, _70_, _80_, 90, _100_ (orange)
f. 35, _40_, 45, _50_, _55_ (yellow)
g. 40, _50_, _60_, 70, _80_ (orange)
h. 70, _75_, 80, _85_, _90_ (yellow)

Bonus Box: 25, 40, 50, 55, 70, 80, 90, 100

Page 118

a. _2_, _4_, 6, _8_, _10_, 12
b. (5), _10_, (15), _20_, (25), _30_
c. _10_, 20, _30_, 40, _50_, _60_, 70
d. (5), 10, (15), _20_, (25), 30, (35)
e. 8, 10, _12_, 14, _16_, 18, _20_
f. 30, 40, _50_, _60_, 70, _80_, _90_
g. (25), 30, (35), _40_, (45), 50

Bonus Box: The odd numbers should be circled as indicated. Written answers will vary.

Page 120

1. 3	7. 2
2. 2	8. 1
3. 2	9. 2
4. 3	10. 3
5. 3	11. 2
6. 1	12. 3

Bonus Box: 2 + 4 = 6. Drawings will vary.

Page 122

1. a. 4, b. 6
2.
3. a. 4, b. 2
4. 2
5. The peppermint sticks should be colored red.
6. The wrapped candies and the lollipops should be colored orange.
7. The candy bars should be colored yellow.

Bonus Box: Two more candy bars are needed to equal the number of lollipops.

Page 124

1. blue
2. green
3. 2
4. 7

Bonus Box: 6, 4 + 2 = 6. Drawings will vary.

Page 126

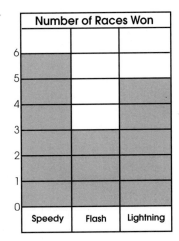

1. 4
2. 6
3. ⊞⊞ ⊞⊞
4. ⊞⊞

Bonus Box: Answers will vary.

Page 128

Number of Races Won		Total
Speedy	⊞⊞ I	6
Flash	III	3
Lightning	⊞⊞	5

Number of Races Won			
6			
5			
4			
3			
2			
1			
0	Speedy	Flash	Lightning

1. Speedy
2. Flash
3. 5, 1
4. 14

Bonus Box: 6 + 5 = 11

Page 130

Part 1: 6, 2. Predictions and colored blocks will vary.
Part 2: Answers to the first 3 questions will vary. One possible explanation for the last question is that there are more spotted than striped cards.

Bonus Box: Students should have drawn 8 cards. The drawings will vary. However, there should be more striped than spotted cards.

Page 132

A. 1 dog, 2 lizard, 3 rabbit
B. 1 bird, 2 guinea pig, 3 cat
C. 1 frog, 2 hamster, 3 turtle

Bonus Box: Answers will vary.

Page 134

Answers may vary. Accept reasonable responses.

1. These shapes belong together because <u>they each have 3 dots.</u> Yes.
2. These shapes belong together because <u>they each have 4 sides.</u> No.
3. These shapes belong together because <u>they are all circles.</u> No.
4. These shapes belong together because <u>they are each divided in half.</u> Yes.

Bonus Box: Answers will vary.

Page 136

1. 6
2. 5
3. 4
4. 2
5. 2
6. 6

Bonus Box: 4 + 2 = 6

Page 138

Cubs: Chin, Sam
Black Bears: Jon, Ann, Lucy, Bill
Grizzlies: Sue, Joy

Bonus Box: The Grizzlies need 2 more players.

Page 140

1. 6
2. 2
3. 6
4. 12

Bonus Box: There would be 4 horses.

Page 142

Drawings will vary.

1. 6
2. 3
3. 7
4. 11

Bonus Box: 18. Drawings will vary.

Page 144

Larry's Lemonade				
Monday	Tuesday	Wednesday	Thursday	Friday
5¢	10¢	5¢	10¢	5¢

Kaila's Cookies				
Monday	Tuesday	Wednesday	Thursday	Friday
5¢	10¢	15¢	20¢	25¢

1. Kaila, 20¢
2. Answers will vary. Possible answers:
   Larry's pattern: It is an ABAB pattern with 5¢ and 10¢.
   Kaila's pattern: Each day, Kaila makes 5¢ more.

Bonus Box:

Larry's Lemonade						
Monday	Tuesday	Wednesday	Thursday	Friday	Saturday	Sunday
5¢	10¢	5¢	10¢	5¢	10¢	5¢

Page 146

The order of the answers may vary.
A. 4. SC, 5. SV, 6. VS
B. 1. purple shirt, red shorts; 2. purple shirt, blue shorts; 3. yellow shirt, red shorts; 4. yellow shirt, blue shorts
C. 3. JR, 4. JC, 5. CR, 6. CJ

Bonus Box: The pictures should represent these possible combinations: hot dog, fries; hot dog, onion rings; hamburger, fries; hamburger, onion rings.

Page 148

Guests	1	2	3	4	5	6
Cookies						

1. 8   2. 12   3. 4

Bonus Box:

Guests	1	2	3	4
Cookies				

Page 150

1. 10

Hours	1	2	3	4	5
Boxes of Doughnuts	2	4	6	8	10

2. 50¢

Doughnuts	1	2	3	4	5
Cost	10¢	20¢	30¢	40¢	50¢

3. 8

Minutes	2	4	6	8	10
Doughnuts	5	10	15	20	25

Bonus Box: 7

174

Page 152

1. yellow, orange
2. orange, red
3. red, yellow
4. red, red
5. orange, orange
6. yellow, yellow, yellow

Bonus Box: orange, yellow, yellow

Page 154

A. 6 (+) 3 = 9
B. 11 (−) 4 = 7
C. 6 (−) 2 = 4
D. 7 (+) 5 = 12
E. 6 (+) 5 = 11
F. 10 (−) 3 = 7

Bonus Box: Answers will vary.

Page 156

1. make a list, 6
   tag, baseball, cards
   tag, cards, baseball
   baseball, tag, cards
   baseball, cards, tag
   cards, baseball, tag
   cards, tag, baseball
2. write a number sentence, 7, 3 + 4 = 7
3. draw a picture, 14
   Drawings will vary. One possible drawing is shown below.

   X   X   X   X   X   X   X
   OO OO OO OO OO OO OO

4. make a table, 12

Mon.	Tues.	Wed.	Thurs.	Fri.	Sat.
2	4	6	8	10	12

Bonus Box: Answers will vary.

Page 158

1. 10
   Drawings will vary. One possible drawing is shown below.

2. 7, 2 + 2 + 3 = 7
3. The first flower should be colored.
4. 9

Mon.	Tues.	Wed.	Thurs.	Fri.
1	3	5	7	9

Bonus Box: Answers will vary, but they should reflect that each day Skunk picks 2 more flowers than he did on the previous day.

Notes

Notes